SCOTT FORESMAN · ADDISON WESLEY

Mathematics

Grade 1

Problem Solving Masters/Workbook

PEARSON

Scott Foresman

Editorial Offices: Glenview, Illinois • Parsippany, New Jersey • New York, New York

Sales Offices: Needham, Massachusetts • Duluth, Georgia • Glenview, Illinois
Coppell, Texas • Ontario, California • Mesa, Arizona

ISBN 0-328-11684-X

18 19

Making 6

You can show 6 in different ways.
Draw the missing coins.
Write the numbers that shows ways to make 6.

1.

<u>2</u>   and   <u>4</u>

2.

_____   and   _____

3.

_____   and   _____

4. Jake has 6 coins.
Can he put the same number
of coins in each bank?

yes   no

Making 7

Macy is having a birthday party.
She needs 7 of each.
Write how many more she needs to make 7.

Macy has		Macy needs
1. 6		_____ more
2. 7		_____ more
3. 2		_____ more
4. 5		_____ more

Macy is making party bags.
She needs 7 of each.
Write how many more she needs to make 7.

Macy has		Macy needs
5. 1		_____ more
6. 5		_____ more
7. 4		_____ more
8. 3		_____ more

Making 8 and 9

What did Meg see on the flower?
Color the ways to make 8 blue.
Color the ways to make 9 yellow.

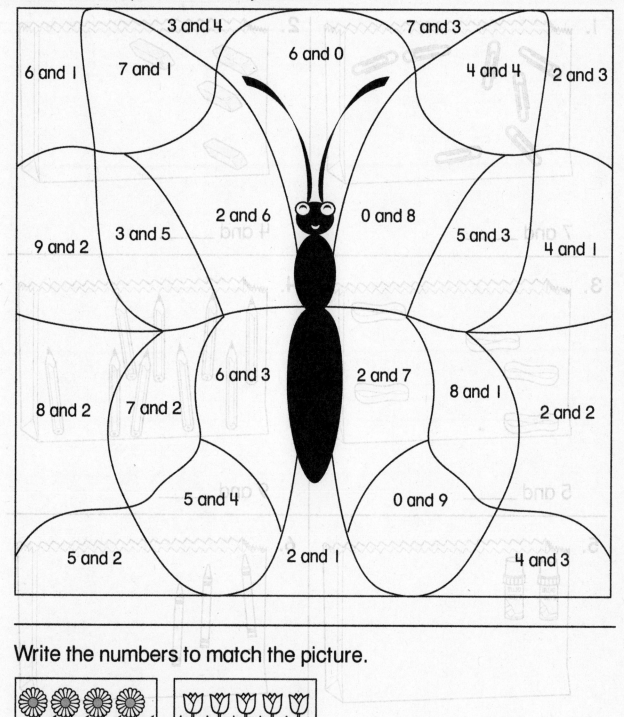

Write the numbers to match the picture.

_____ and _____

Making 10

Each bag needs 10 items.
Draw the missing items to make 10.
Write the numbers that show ways to make 10.

1.

7 and _____

2.

4 and _____

3.

5 and _____

4.

9 and _____

5.

2 and _____

6.

3 and _____

PROBLEM-SOLVING STRATEGY

Use Objects

Lynn is planting 11 flowers in 2 flower boxes.
She will put some flowers in each box.
In what different ways can she put the flowers?

Use paper for
flower boxes.
Use counters for
the flowers.

__6__ and __5__

What other ways can you put 11 flowers into
2 flower boxes?

1. _____ and _____

2. _____ and _____

3. _____ and _____

4. _____ and _____

5. _____ and _____

Using the page Ask children to *look back and check* their work to make sure they used all of the
11 counters with some counters on each paper.

1 and 2 More Than

Draw 1 or 2 more.
Write the numbers.

1.

6 and 1 more is _____.

2.

8 and 2 more is _____.

3.

4 and 1 more is _____.

4.

5 and 2 more is _____.

5.

7 and 2 more is _____.

6.

3 and 2 more is _____.

Write the numbers.

7. 4 and _____ more is 5.

8. 9 and _____ more is 10.

9. 5 and _____ more is 7.

10. 7 and _____ more is 9.

1 and 2 Fewer Than

Find 1 or 2 fewer than.

Cross out the objects. Write the numbers.

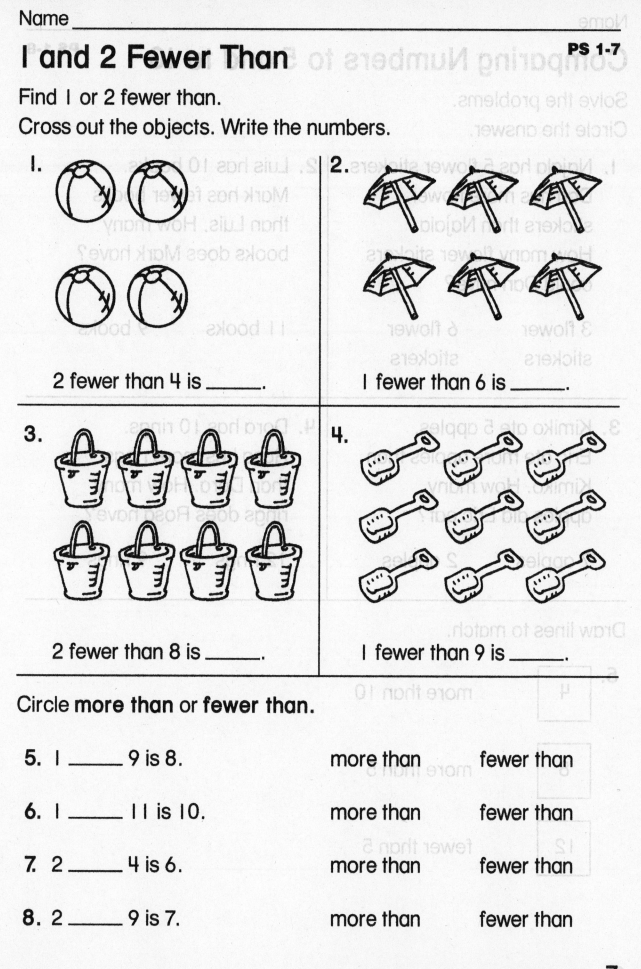

1.

2 fewer than 4 is _____.

2.

1 fewer than 6 is _____.

3.

2 fewer than 8 is _____.

4.

1 fewer than 9 is _____.

Circle **more than** or **fewer than**.

5. 1 _____ 9 is 8.   more than   fewer than

6. 1 _____ 11 is 10.   more than   fewer than

7. 2 _____ 4 is 6.   more than   fewer than

8. 2 _____ 9 is 7.   more than   fewer than

Comparing Numbers to 5 and to 10

Solve the problems.
Circle the answer.

1. Najala has 5 flower stickers. Dan has more flower stickers than Najala. How many flower stickers could Dan have?

   3 flower   6 flower
   stickers   stickers

2. Luis has 10 books. Mark has fewer books than Luis. How many books does Mark have?

   11 books   9 books

3. Kimiko ate 5 apples. Eric ate more apples than Kimiko. How many apples did Eric eat?

   7 apples   2 apples

4. Dora has 10 rings. Rosa has more rings than Dora. How many rings does Rosa have?

   12 rings   9 rings

Draw lines to match.

5.

4	more than 10
8	more than 5
12	fewer than 5

Ordering Numbers Through 12

Answer each question. Write the numbers
in order from least to greatest.

1. Dee, Mario, and Sal spin to go first.
   Dee spins a 7. Mario spins a 3. Sal spins an 8.
   The person with the least number goes first.

   Who goes first? _____   __3__ , __7__ , __8__
                                    least   greatest

2. On the first turn, Mario spins a 5.
   Dee spins a 9. Sal spins a 7.   _____ , _____ , _____
                                          least   greatest

   Who spins the greatest number? _____

   Who spins the least number? _____

3. Sal spins again. Sal spins a 4.
   Dee spins an 8. Mario spins an 11.   _____ , _____ , _____
                                          least   greatest

   Who spins the greatest number? _____

   Who spins the least number? _____

4. On their last turn, Sal spins a 9.
   Dee spins a 7. Mario spins an 8.   _____ , _____ , _____
                                          least   greatest

   Who spins the greatest number? _____

   Who spins the least number? _____

Identifying the Pattern Unit

Beads fell off of the necklaces.
Draw what is missing.

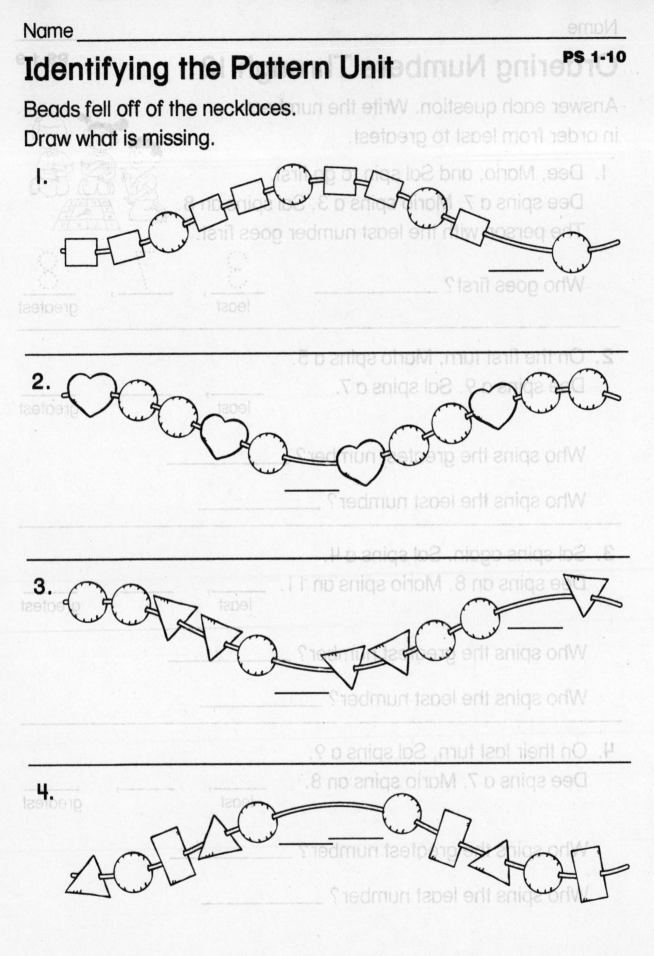

1.

2.

3.

4.

Translating Patterns

Draw a pattern to match the letter pattern.

1.

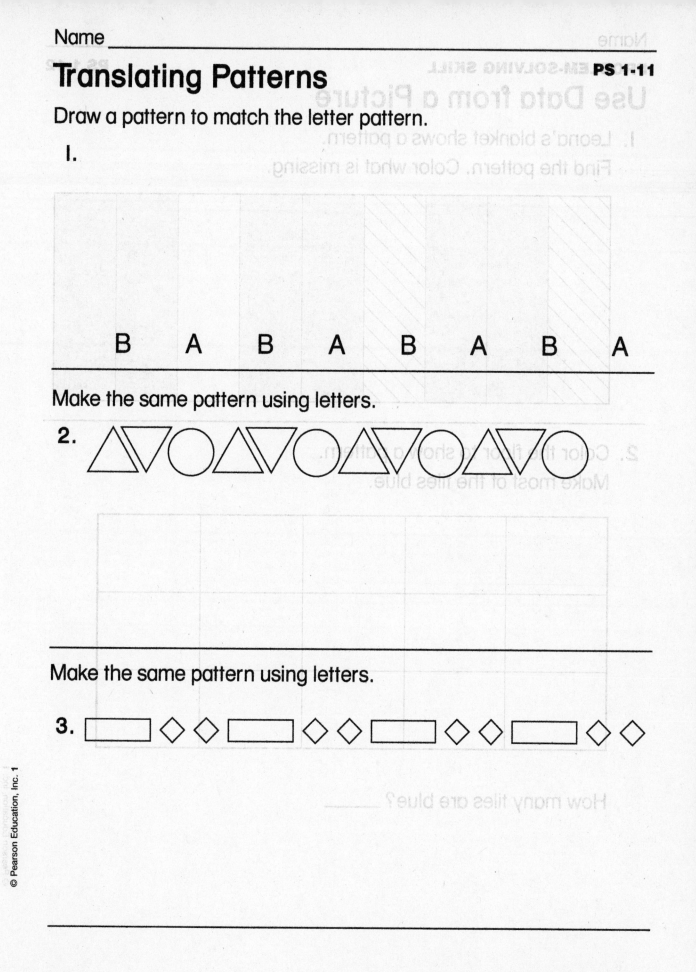

B   A   B   A   B   A   B   A   B   A

Make the same pattern using letters.

2.

Make the same pattern using letters.

3.

PROBLEM-SOLVING SKILL
Use Data from a Picture

1. Leona's blanket shows a pattern.

Find the pattern. Color what is missing.

2. Color the floor to show a pattern.

Make most of the tiles blue.

How many tiles are blue? _____

PROBLEM-SOLVING APPLICATIONS

It's a Party!

1. Color the beads and shells to show a pattern.
   Draw and color what comes next.

_____

2. If you put 1 more bead onto the necklace,
   how many beads will there be?

   8 and 1 more is _____.

_____

3. Sydney wants to put 9 shells on a necklace.
   She has 3 shells.
   How many more shells does she need?

   _____ more shells

_____

4. Elena has 7 beads.
   Pam has 5 beads.
   How many fewer beads does Pam have?

   Pam has _____ fewer beads.

_____

Using the page Have children read the exercises several times. To help children *understand,* ask them to tell what they know and what they must find out.

Name _____

Stories about Joining

Use counters to answer each question.

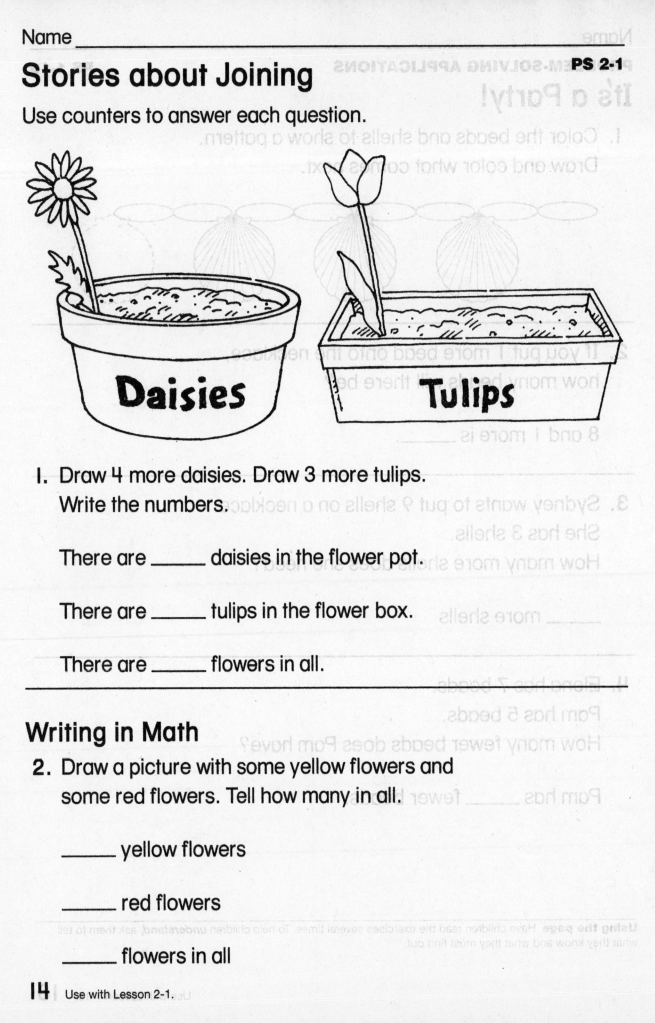

1. Draw 4 more daisies. Draw 3 more tulips.
   Write the numbers.

   There are _____ daisies in the flower pot.

   There are _____ tulips in the flower box.

   There are _____ flowers in all.

Writing in Math

2. Draw a picture with some yellow flowers and
   some red flowers. Tell how many in all.

   _____ yellow flowers

   _____ red flowers

   _____ flowers in all

© Pearson Education, Inc. 1

Using Counters to Add

Use the picture to answer the question.
Write **more** or **less**.

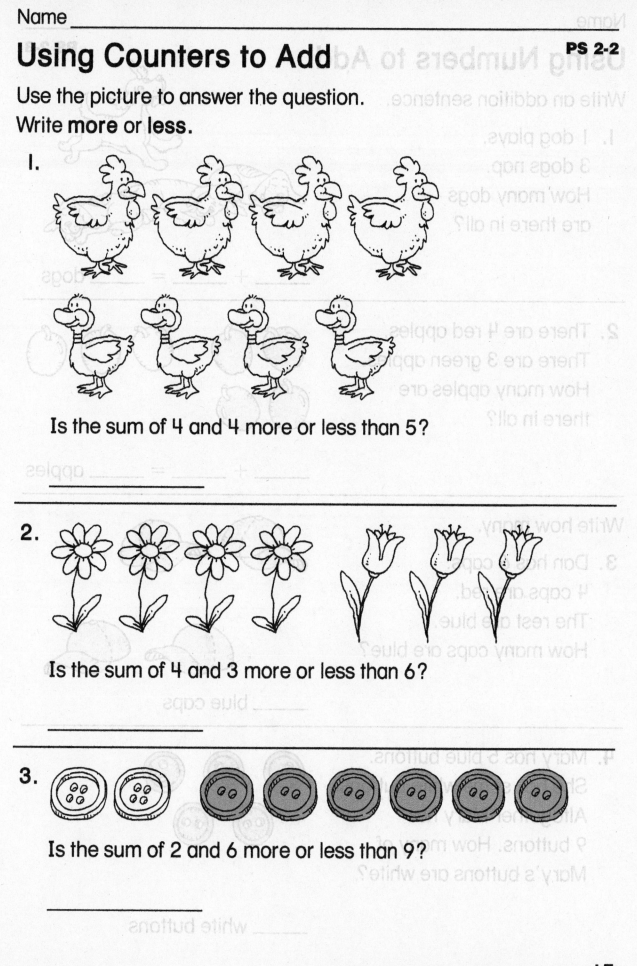

1.

Is the sum of 4 and 4 more or less than 5?

_____

2.

Is the sum of 4 and 3 more or less than 6?

_____

3.

Is the sum of 2 and 6 more or less than 9?

_____

Using Numbers to Add

Write an addition sentence.

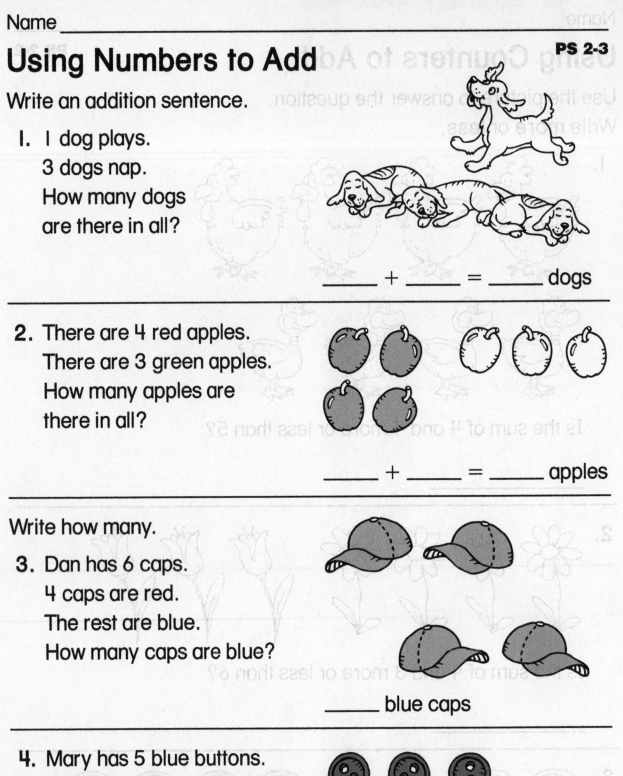

1. 1 dog plays.

3 dogs nap.

How many dogs
are there in all?

_____ + _____ = _____ dogs

2. There are 4 red apples.

There are 3 green apples.

How many apples are
there in all?

_____ + _____ = _____ apples

Write how many.

3. Dan has 6 caps.

4 caps are red.

The rest are blue.

How many caps are blue?

_____ blue caps

4. Mary has 5 blue buttons.

She has some white buttons.

Altogether Mary has

9 buttons. How many of
Mary's buttons are white?

_____ white buttons

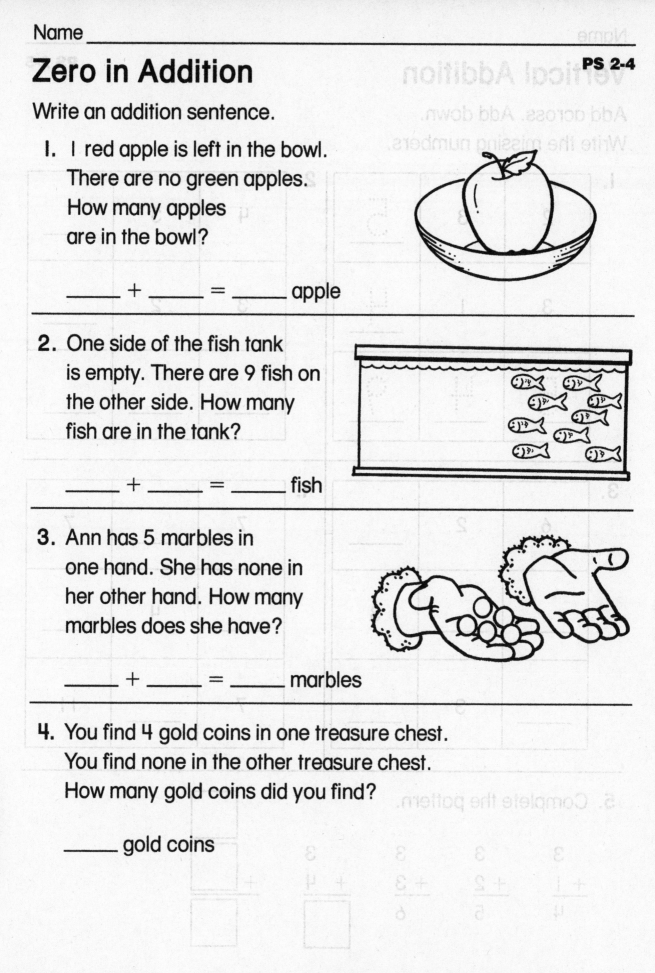

Zero in Addition

Write an addition sentence.

1. 1 red apple is left in the bowl.
   There are no green apples.
   How many apples
   are in the bowl?

   _____ + _____ = _____ apple

2. One side of the fish tank
   is empty. There are 9 fish on
   the other side. How many
   fish are in the tank?

   _____ + _____ = _____ fish

3. Ann has 5 marbles in
   one hand. She has none in
   her other hand. How many
   marbles does she have?

   _____ + _____ = _____ marbles

4. You find 4 gold coins in one treasure chest.
   You find none in the other treasure chest.
   How many gold coins did you find?

   _____ gold coins

Name

Vertical Addition

PS 2-5

Add across. Add down.
Write the missing numbers.

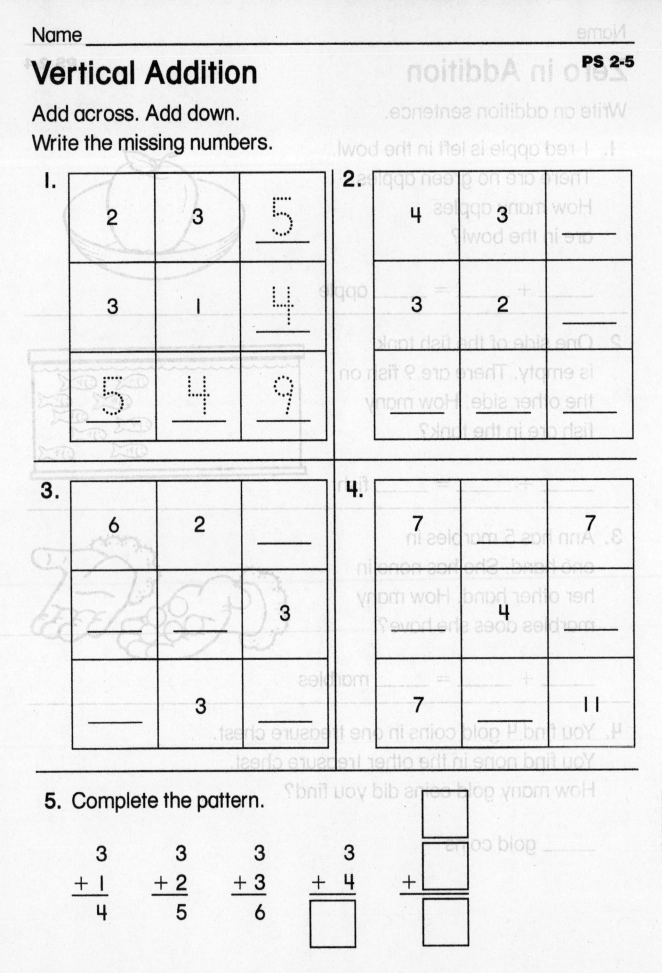

1.

2	3	5
3	1	4
5	4	9

2.

4	3	___
3	2	___
		___

3.

6	2	___
___	___	3
___	3	___

4.

7	___	7
	4	
7	___	11

5. Complete the pattern.

$$3 \atop \underline{+\,1} \atop 4 \qquad 3 \atop \underline{+\,2} \atop 5 \qquad 3 \atop \underline{+\,3} \atop 6 \qquad 3 \atop \underline{+\,4} \atop \boxed{} \qquad 3 \atop \underline{+\,\boxed{}} \atop \boxed{}$$

© Pearson Education, Inc. 1

PROBLEM-SOLVING STRATEGY PS 2-6

Write a Number Sentence

3 children are playing.

5 more children come to play.

How many children are playing in all?

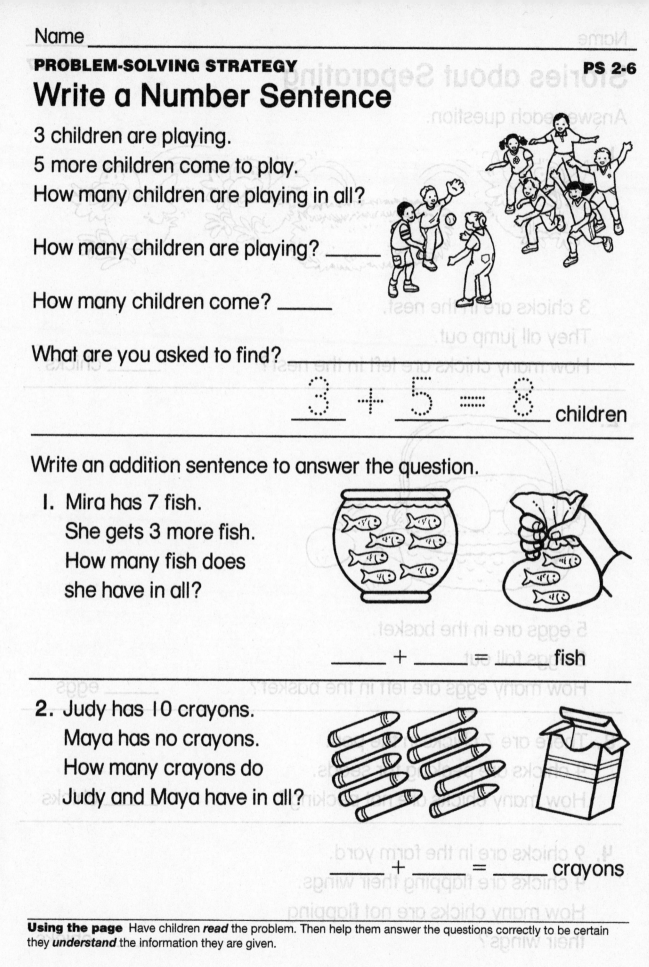

How many children are playing? _____

How many children come? _____

What are you asked to find? _____

$$\underline{3} + \underline{5} = \underline{8} \text{ children}$$

Write an addition sentence to answer the question.

1. Mira has 7 fish.
   She gets 3 more fish.
   How many fish does
   she have in all?

   _____ + _____ = _____ fish

2. Judy has 10 crayons.
   Maya has no crayons.
   How many crayons do
   Judy and Maya have in all?

   _____ + _____ = _____ crayons

Using the page Have children *read* the problem. Then help them answer the questions correctly to be certain they *understand* the information they are given.

Stories about Separating

Answer each question.

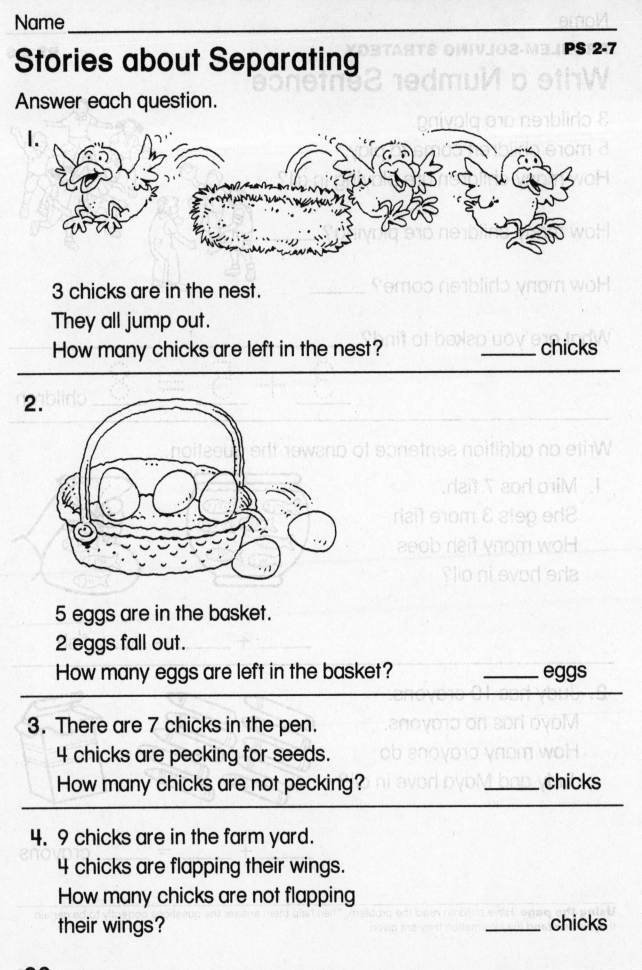

1.

3 chicks are in the nest.

They all jump out.

How many chicks are left in the nest? _____ chicks

2.

5 eggs are in the basket.

2 eggs fall out.

How many eggs are left in the basket? _____ eggs

3. There are 7 chicks in the pen.

4 chicks are pecking for seeds.

How many chicks are not pecking? _____ chicks

4. 9 chicks are in the farm yard.

4 chicks are flapping their wings.

How many chicks are not flapping
their wings? _____ chicks

Using Counters to Subtract

Write how many in the basket.
Circle what you want to take away.
Write how many are left in the basket.

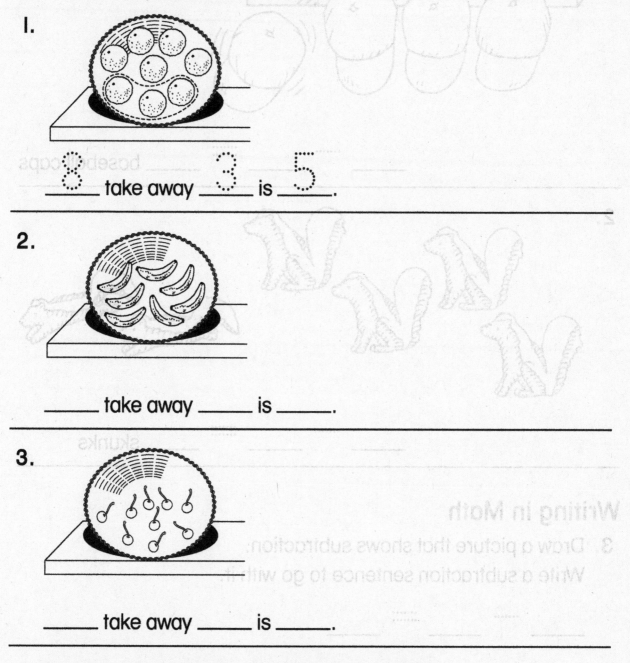

1.

8 take away 3 is 5 .

2.

_____ take away _____ is _____ .

3.

_____ take away _____ is _____ .

4. Draw a picture to show the greatest number
of apples you can take away from 6 apples.

Using Numbers to Subtract

Write a subtraction sentence.

1.

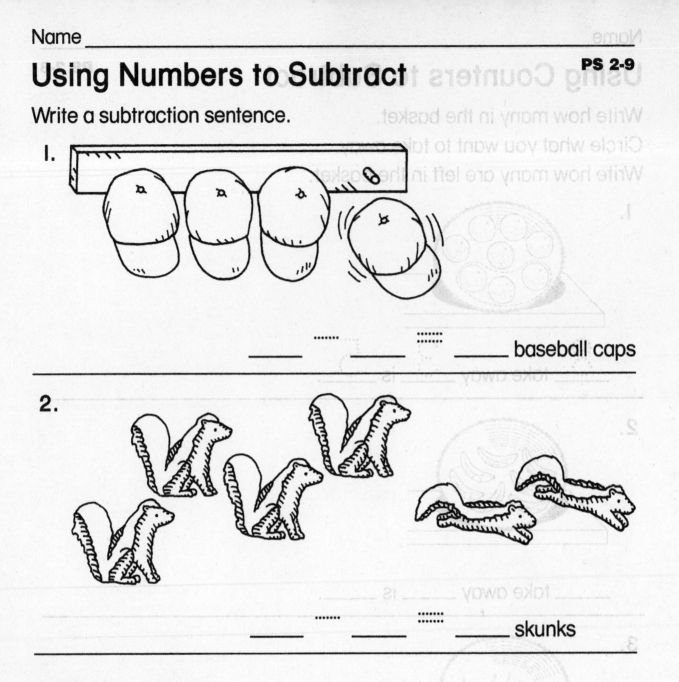

_____ _____ _____ baseball caps

2.

_____ _____ _____ skunks

Writing in Math

3. Draw a picture that shows subtraction.
Write a subtraction sentence to go with it.

_____ _____ _____

Zero in Subtraction

Write the missing numbers to finish the subtraction sentences.

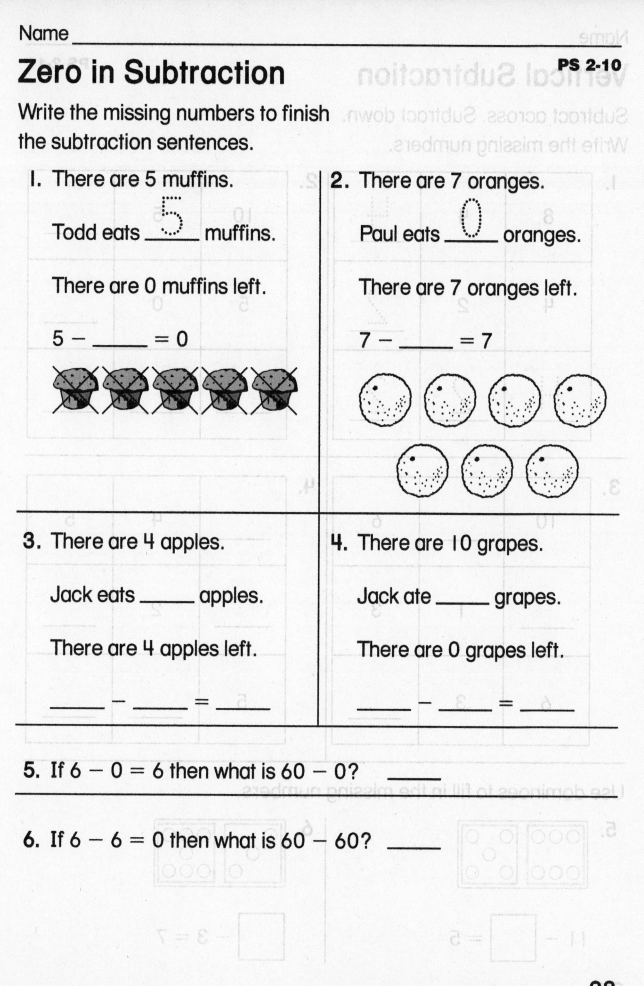

1. There are 5 muffins.

Todd eats __5__ muffins.

There are 0 muffins left.

5 − _____ = 0

2. There are 7 oranges.

Paul eats __0__ oranges.

There are 7 oranges left.

7 − _____ = 7

3. There are 4 apples.

Jack eats _____ apples.

There are 4 apples left.

_____ − _____ = _____

4. There are 10 grapes.

Jack ate _____ grapes.

There are 0 grapes left.

_____ − _____ = _____

5. If 6 − 0 = 6 then what is 60 − 0? _____

6. If 6 − 6 = 0 then what is 60 − 60? _____

Vertical Subtraction

Subtract across. Subtract down.
Write the missing numbers.

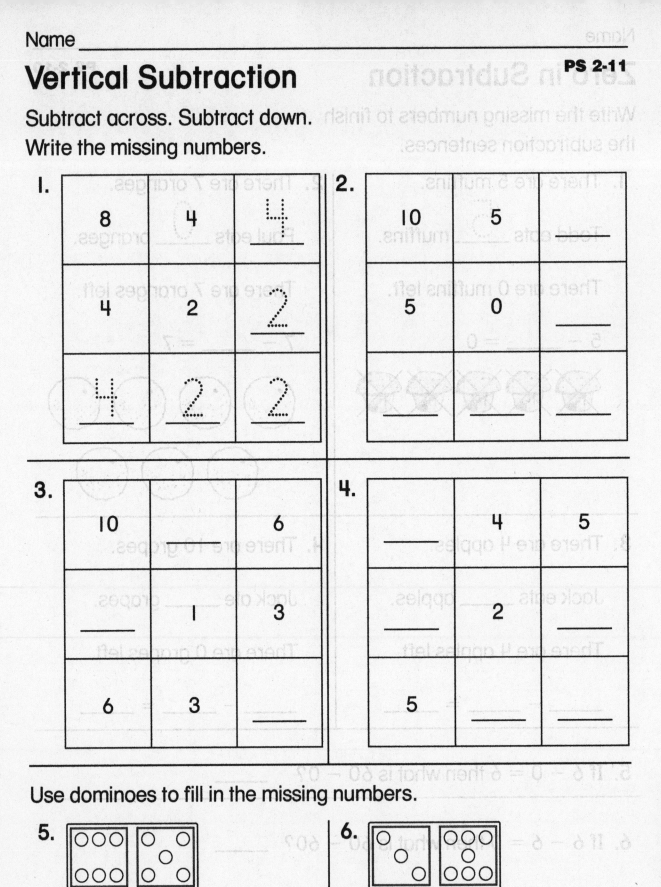

1.

8	4	4
4	2	2
4	2	2

2.

10	5	___
5	0	___
___	___	___

3.

10		6
___	1	3
6	3	___

4.

	4	5
___	2	___
5	___	___

Use dominoes to fill in the missing numbers.

5.

$11 - \boxed{} = 5$

6.

$\boxed{} - 3 = 7$

PROBLEM-SOLVING SKILL

Choose an Operation

Use the picture. Choose **add** or **subtract**.

Write the answer.

1. 2 baby whales are swimming with 1 mother whale.

How many whales are there in all?

add   subtract   _____ whales

2. 4 seals are sunbathing. 0 seals leave.

How many seals are still sunbathing?

add   subtract   _____ seals

3. 5 penguins are walking.

3 penguins jump in the water.

How many penguins are still walking?

add   subtract   _____ penguins

Using the page To help children *plan*, discuss whether they will add or subtract to *solve* each problem.

Using Cubes to Compare

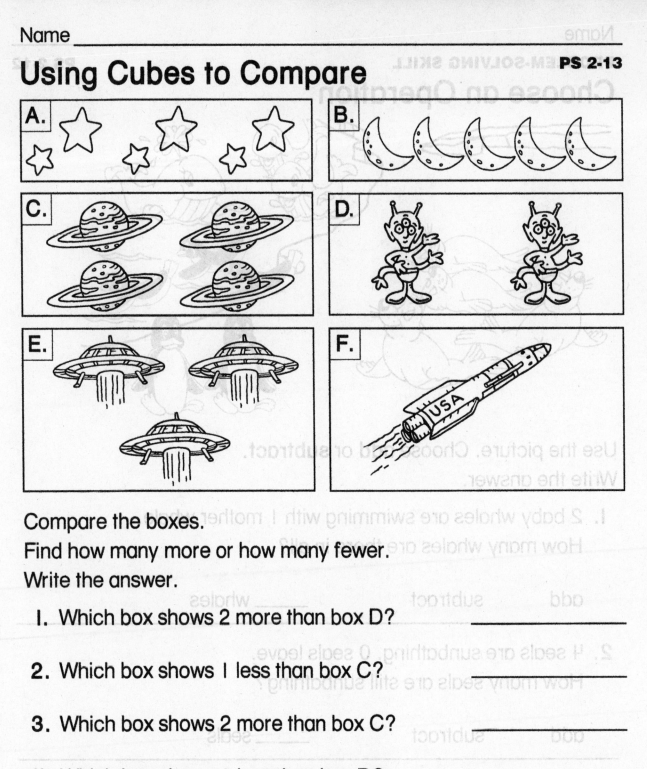

Compare the boxes.

Find how many more or how many fewer.

Write the answer.

1. Which box shows 2 more than box D? _____

2. Which box shows 1 less than box C? _____

3. Which box shows 2 more than box C? _____

4. Which box shows 1 less than box D? _____

5. Which box shows 2 more than box E? _____

6. Which box shows 2 less than box C? _____

7. Which box shows 1 more than box D? _____

Using Subtraction to Compare

Write a subtraction sentence.
Then write how many more or how many fewer.

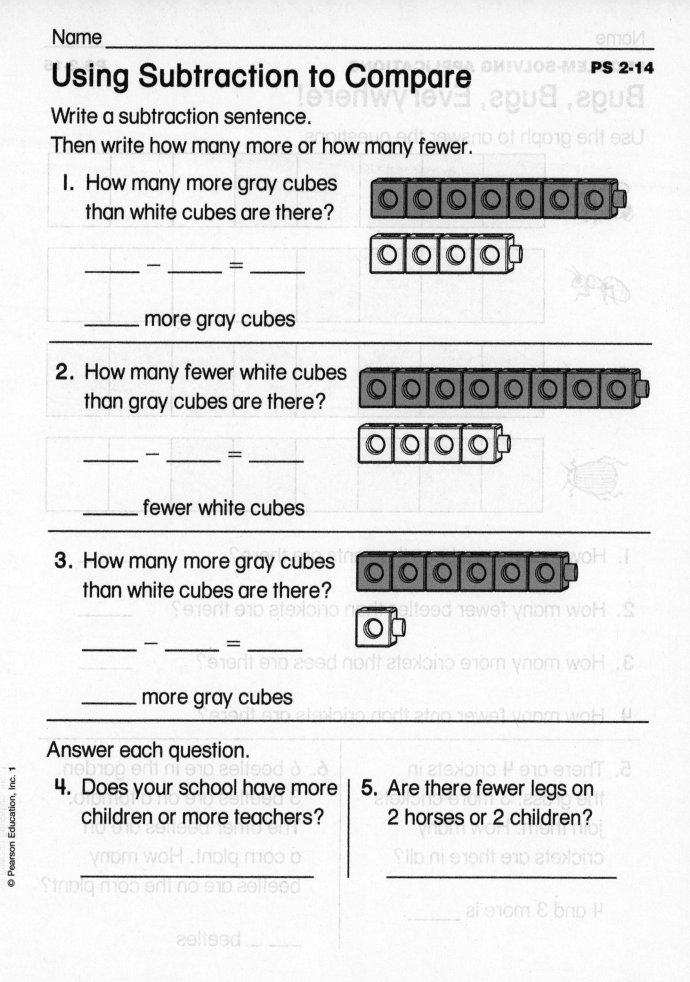

1. How many more gray cubes than white cubes are there?

_____ – _____ = _____

_____ more gray cubes

2. How many fewer white cubes than gray cubes are there?

_____ – _____ = _____

_____ fewer white cubes

3. How many more gray cubes than white cubes are there?

_____ – _____ = _____

_____ more gray cubes

Answer each question.

4. Does your school have more children or more teachers?

_____

5. Are there fewer legs on 2 horses or 2 children?

_____

PROBLEM-SOLVING APPLICATIONS   **PS 2-15**

Bugs, Bugs, Everywhere!

Use the graph to answer the questions.

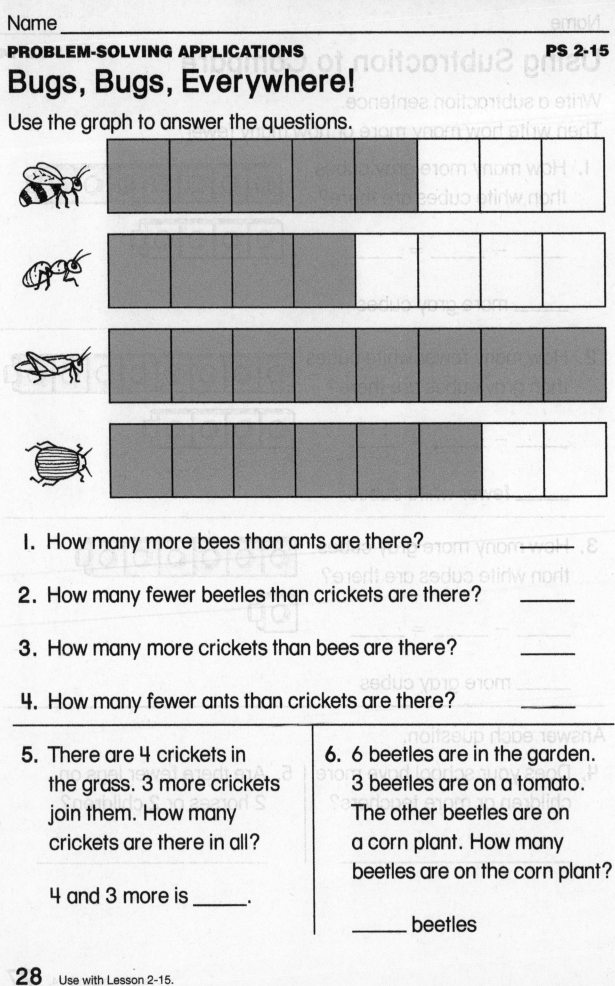

1. How many more bees than ants are there? _____

2. How many fewer beetles than crickets are there? _____

3. How many more crickets than bees are there? _____

4. How many fewer ants than crickets are there? _____

5. There are 4 crickets in the grass. 3 more crickets join them. How many crickets are there in all?

   4 and 3 more is _____.

6. 6 beetles are in the garden. 3 beetles are on a tomato. The other beetles are on a corn plant. How many beetles are on the corn plant?

   _____ beetles

Counting On 1, 2, or 3

Write the numbers. Count on to solve.

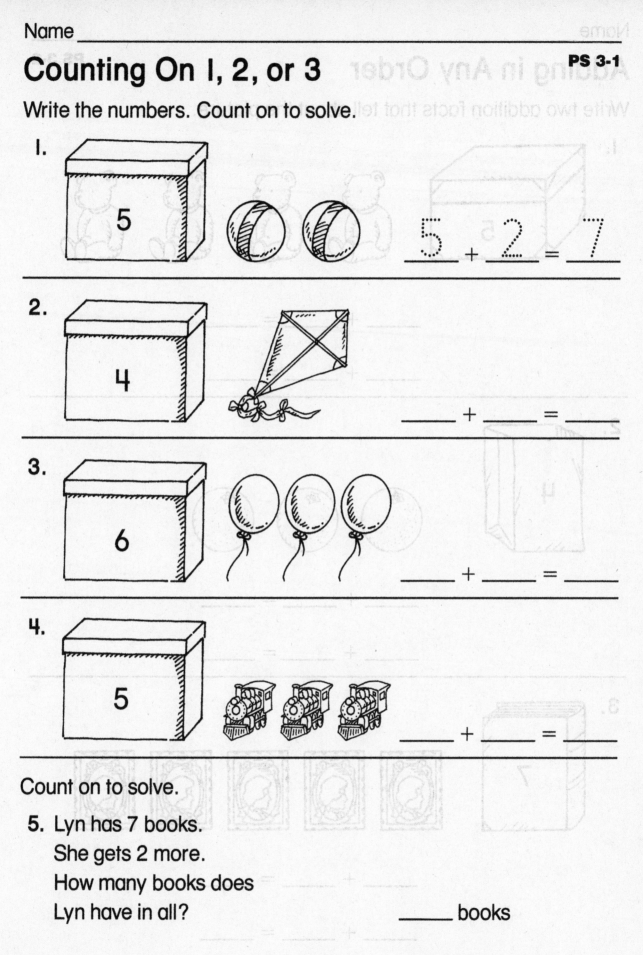

1. 5 $5 + 2 = 7$

2. 4   _____ + _____ = _____

3. 6   _____ + _____ = _____

4. 5   _____ + _____ = _____

Count on to solve.

5. Lyn has 7 books.
   She gets 2 more.
   How many books does
   Lyn have in all?   _____ books

Adding in Any Order

Write two addition facts that tell about the picture.

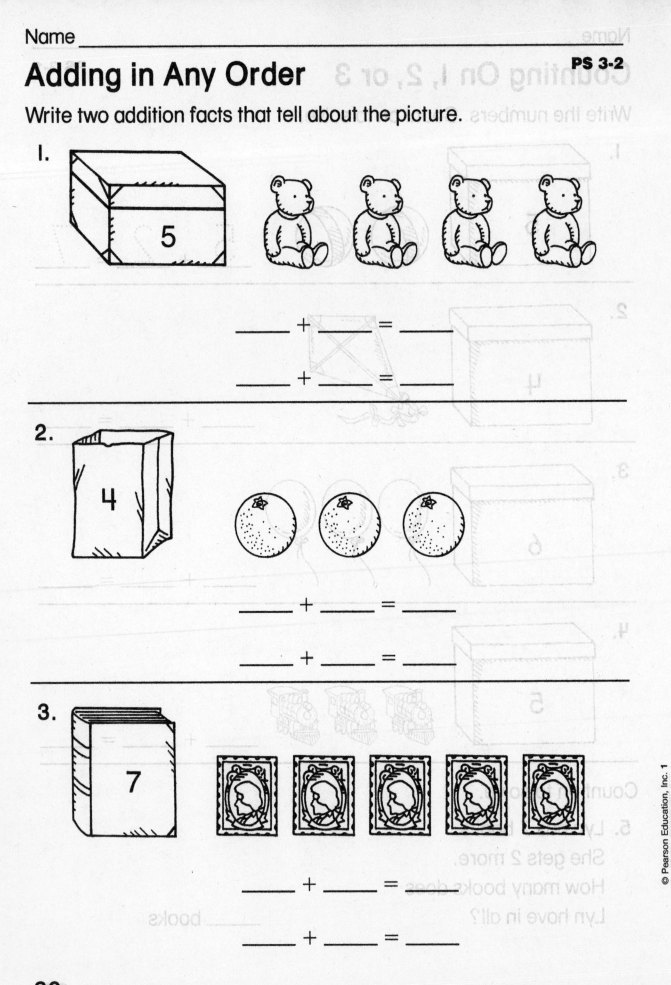

1. [box: 5] [4 bears]

_____ + _____ = _____

_____ + _____ = _____

2. [bag: 4] [3 oranges]

_____ + _____ = _____

_____ + _____ = _____

3. [book: 7] [5 stamps]

_____ + _____ = _____

_____ + _____ = _____

Adding 1, 2, or 3

Finish the picture and complete
the addition sentence.

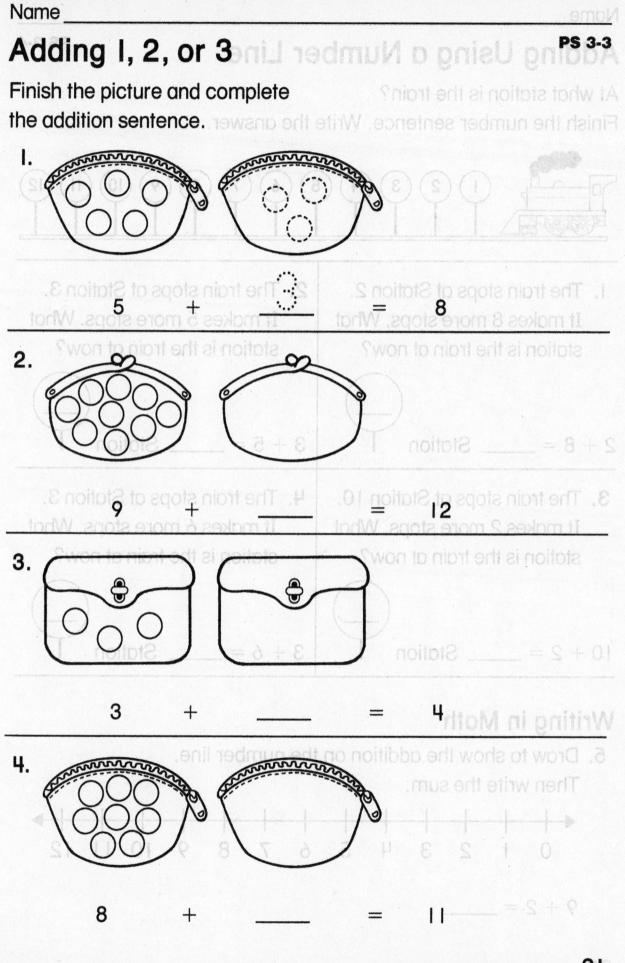

1.

$$5 + \underline{} = 8$$

2.

$$9 + \underline{} = 12$$

3.

$$3 + \underline{} = 4$$

4.

$$8 + \underline{} = 11$$

Adding Using a Number Line

At what station is the train?
Finish the number sentence. Write the answer.

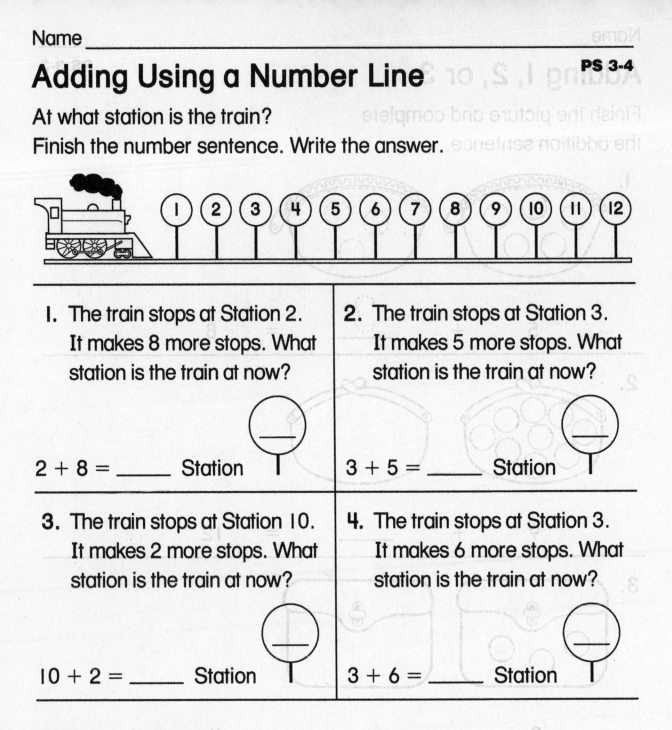

1. The train stops at Station 2. It makes 8 more stops. What station is the train at now?

2 + 8 = _____ Station

2. The train stops at Station 3. It makes 5 more stops. What station is the train at now?

3 + 5 = _____ Station

3. The train stops at Station 10. It makes 2 more stops. What station is the train at now?

10 + 2 = _____ Station

4. The train stops at Station 3. It makes 6 more stops. What station is the train at now?

3 + 6 = _____ Station

Writing in Math

5. Draw to show the addition on the number line. Then write the sum.

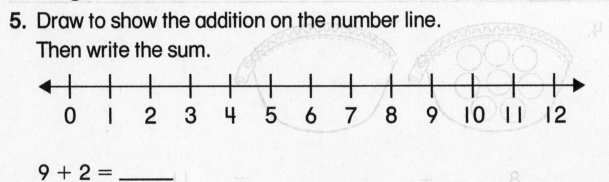

9 + 2 = _____

© Pearson Education, Inc. 1

Name _____

Extra Information

2 children ride red bikes.

~~4 children play tag.~~

3 children ride green bikes.

(How many children ride bikes?)

Circle what you
are asked to find.

What you need:

Cross out any
extra information.

___2___ children ride red bikes.

___3___ children ride green bikes.

___2___ + ___3___ = ___5___ children

Cross out the extra information.

Then write a number sentence to solve the problem.

I. 6 children are at the park.
   3 children meet them.
   They watch 4 dogs play.
   How many children are
   at the park?

   _____ + _____ = _____ children

---

2. There are 7 red buckets.
   There are 5 blue shovels.
   There is I blue bucket.
   How many buckets
   are there?

   _____ + _____ = _____ buckets

Using the page Have children *read* the exercise and identify what they are asked to find. Then help
them *understand* how to find the information needed to solve the exercise.

Doubles

Kim and Tim are twins.
Kim has the same number of objects as Tim.
Write an addition sentence.

1. Tim has 2 green hats.
How many green hats do
the twins have altogether?

__2__ + __2__ = __4__ hats

2. Tim has 4 books.
How many books do the
twins have altogether?

_____ + _____ = _____ books

3. Tim has 5 crayons.
How many crayons do the
twins have in all?

_____ + _____ = _____ crayons

4. Tim has 6 stamps.
How many stamps do the
twins have altogether?

_____ + _____ = _____ stamps

Write a number sentence to answer the question.

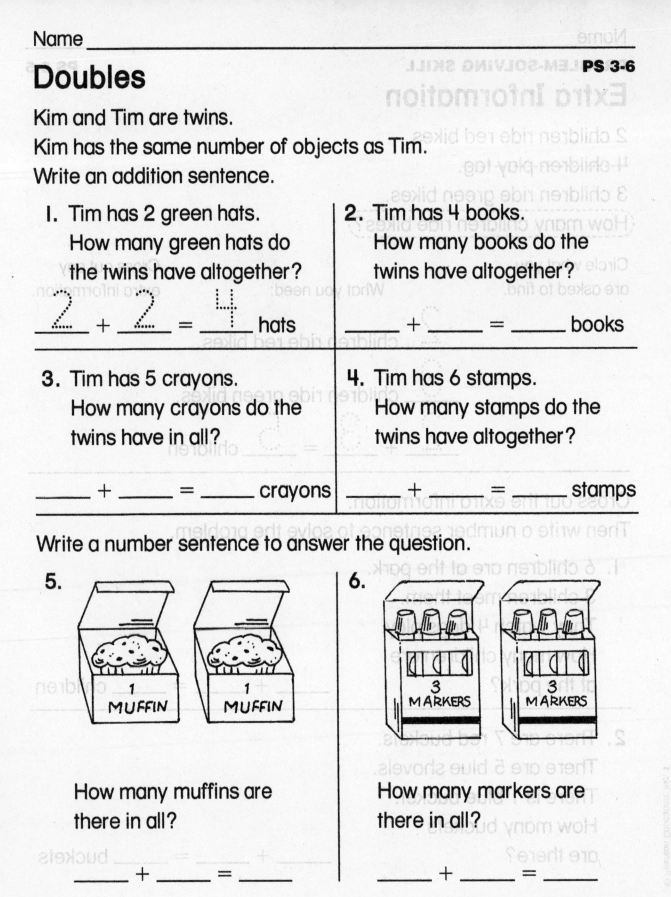

5.

How many muffins are
there in all?

_____ + _____ = _____

6.

How many markers are
there in all?

_____ + _____ = _____

Doubles Plus 1

Use the domino to solve the riddle.

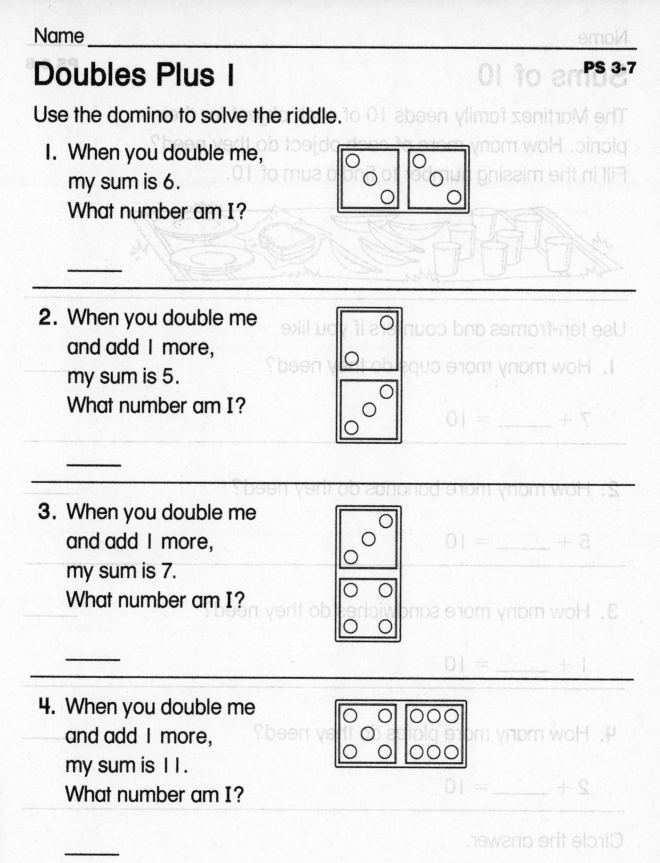

1. When you double me,
   my sum is 6.
   What number am I?

   _____

2. When you double me
   and add 1 more,
   my sum is 5.
   What number am I?

   _____

3. When you double me
   and add 1 more,
   my sum is 7.
   What number am I?

   _____

4. When you double me
   and add 1 more,
   my sum is 11.
   What number am I?

   _____

Sums of 10

The Martinez family needs 10 of each object for their
picnic. How many more of each object do they need?
Fill in the missing number to find a sum of 10.

Use ten-frames and counters if you like.

1. How many more cups do they need?

$7 + \underline{\hspace{1cm}} = 10$

2. How many more bananas do they need?

$5 + \underline{\hspace{1cm}} = 10$

3. How many more sandwiches do they need?

$1 + \underline{\hspace{1cm}} = 10$

4. How many more plates do they need?

$2 + \underline{\hspace{1cm}} = 10$

Circle the answer.

5. Dana sees 6 ants.
   How many more must
   she see to make 10?   4   5   6   7

PROBLEM-SOLVING STRATEGY

Draw a Picture

Beth has 6 red balloons.

She buys 4 blue balloons.

How many balloons does Beth have in all?

<u> 6 </u>   +   <u> 4 </u> = <u> 10 </u>

Draw a picture. Then write a number sentence.

1. Jane saw 8 bugs.

    She saw 3 more bugs.

    How many bugs did

    Jane see altogether?

    _____ + _____ = _____ bugs

2. Tom saw 3 fish.

    He saw 9 more fish.

    How many fish did

    Tom see in all?

    _____ + _____ = _____ fish

Using the page Have students **look back and check** that their addition sentence matches the number of objects in their picture.

Name _____

PROBLEM-SOLVING APPLICATIONS
Hop to It!

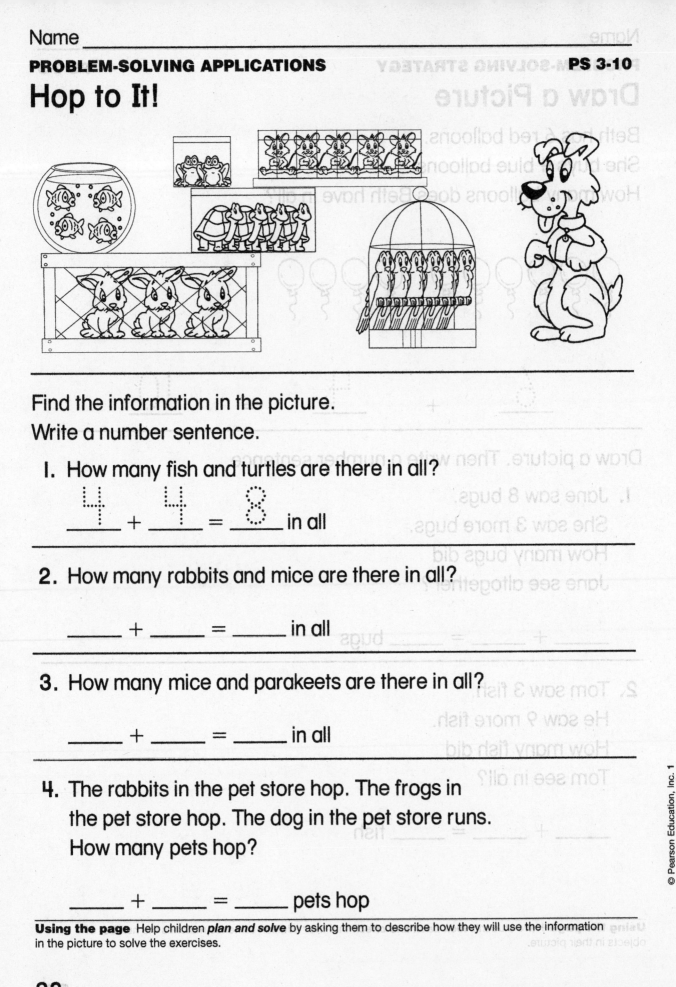

Find the information in the picture.

Write a number sentence.

1. How many fish and turtles are there in all?

    __4__ + __4__ = __8__ in all

2. How many rabbits and mice are there in all?

    _____ + _____ = _____ in all

3. How many mice and parakeets are there in all?

    _____ + _____ = _____ in all

4. The rabbits in the pet store hop. The frogs in
    the pet store hop. The dog in the pet store runs.
    How many pets hop?

    _____ + _____ = _____ pets hop

© Pearson Education, Inc. 1

Using the page Help children *plan and solve* by asking them to describe how they will use the information
in the picture to solve the exercises.

Counting Back Using a Number Line PS 4-1

Write a subtraction sentence for each number line.

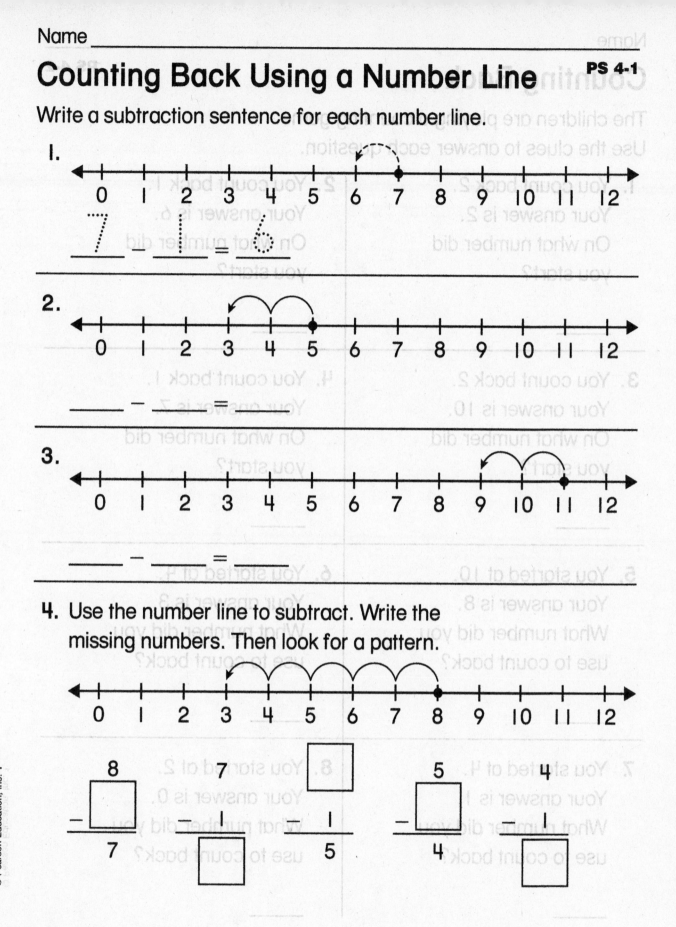

1.

$$7 \quad - \quad 1 \quad = \quad 6$$

2.

_____ − _____ = _____

3.

_____ − _____ = _____

4. Use the number line to subtract. Write the
missing numbers. Then look for a pattern.

$$8 \\ -\ \square \\ \overline{7}$$

$$7 \\ -\ \square \\ \overline{\ }$$

$$\square \\ -\ 1 \\ \overline{5}$$

$$5 \\ -\ \square \\ \overline{4}$$

$$4 \\ -\ 1 \\ \overline{\ }$$

Counting Back

The children are playing a counting game.
Use the clues to answer each question.

1. You count back 2.
   Your answer is 2.
   On what number did
   you start?

   _____

2. You count back 1.
   Your answer is 6.
   On what number did
   you start?

   _____

3. You count back 2.
   Your answer is 10.
   On what number did
   you start?

   _____

4. You count back 1.
   Your answer is 7.
   On what number did
   you start?

   _____

5. You started at 10.
   Your answer is 8.
   What number did you
   use to count back?

   _____

6. You started at 4.
   Your answer is 3.
   What number did you
   use to count back?

   _____

7. You started at 4.
   Your answer is 1.
   What number did you
   use to count back?

   _____

8. You started at 2.
   Your answer is 0.
   What number did you
   use to count back?

   _____

Using Doubles to Subtract

Write an addition sentence and a subtraction sentence.

1.  Mrs. Smith buys 2 cartons of eggs.
How many eggs does she buy in all?

_____ + _____ = _____

 Mrs. Smith cooks 6 eggs.
How many eggs does she have left?

_____ − _____ = _____

2.  Mr. Green buys 2 baskets of apples.
How many apples does he buy?

_____ + _____ = _____

 Mr. Green uses 5 apples to make apple butter.
How many apples does he have left?

_____ − _____ = _____

3. 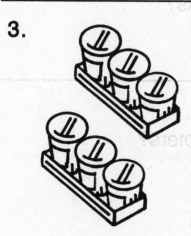 Mrs. Lee buys 2 packs of yogurt.
How many containers of yogurt does she buy?

_____ + _____ = _____

Mrs. Lee's children eat 3 containers of yogurt.
How many containers of yogurt does
Mrs. Lee have left?

_____ − _____ = _____

PROBLEM-SOLVING STRATEGY

Write a Number Sentence

6 girls are drawing on the chalkboard.

2 girls sit down.

How many girls are left at the chalkboard?

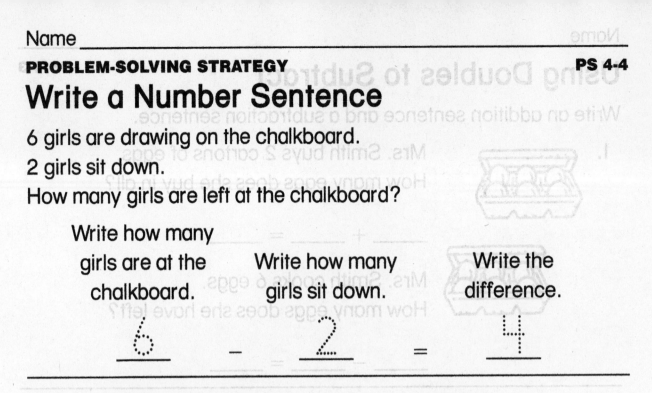

Write how many girls are at the chalkboard.		Write how many girls sit down.		Write the difference.
6	−	2	=	4

Write a subtraction sentence to answer the question.

1. There are 7 boys and 5 girls playing kickball.
   How many more boys than girls are playing?

   ____ − ____ = ____

---

2. There are 10 children eating snacks
   and 4 children playing.
   How many more children are eating snacks?

   ____ − ____ = ____

---

3. There are 7 bikes and 3 scooters.
   How many more bikes are there than scooters?

   ____ − ____ = ____

Using the page To help children *plan,* have them first read each exercise and discuss what it is asking them to find. Then have them write down the number sentence that will *solve* the problem.

Using Related Facts

Fill in the missing numbers.
Then draw lines to match the related addition and
subtraction facts.

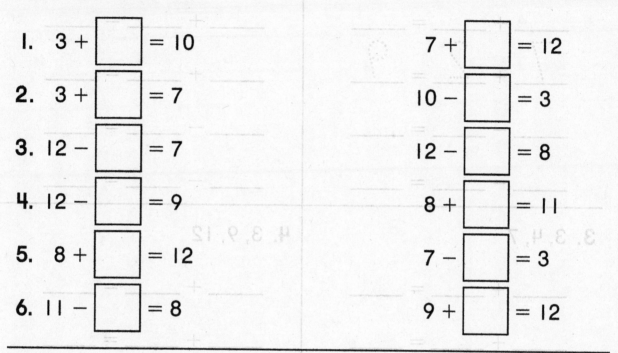

1. $3 + \boxed{} = 10$

2. $3 + \boxed{} = 7$

3. $12 - \boxed{} = 7$

4. $12 - \boxed{} = 9$

5. $8 + \boxed{} = 12$

6. $11 - \boxed{} = 8$

$7 + \boxed{} = 12$

$10 - \boxed{} = 3$

$12 - \boxed{} = 8$

$8 + \boxed{} = 11$

$7 - \boxed{} = 3$

$9 + \boxed{} = 12$

Writing In Math

7. Draw a picture to show the related facts.

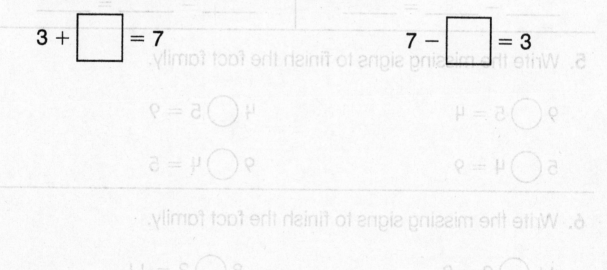

$3 + \boxed{} = 7$ $7 - \boxed{} = 3$

Fact Families

Write each fact family using the numbers.

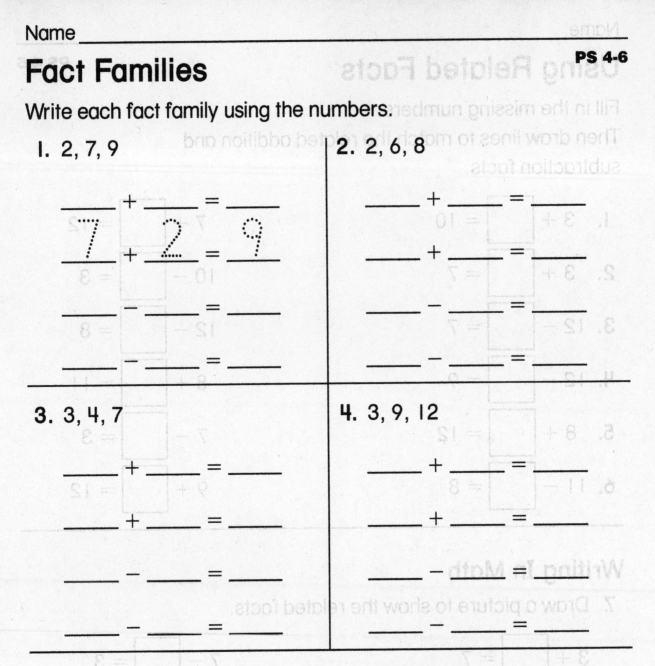

1. 2, 7, 9

_____ + _____ = _____

7 + 2 = 9

_____ + _____ = _____

_____ − _____ = _____

_____ − _____ = _____

2. 2, 6, 8

_____ + _____ = _____

_____ + _____ = _____

_____ − _____ = _____

_____ − _____ = _____

3. 3, 4, 7

_____ + _____ = _____

_____ + _____ = _____

_____ − _____ = _____

_____ − _____ = _____

4. 3, 9, 12

_____ + _____ = _____

_____ + _____ = _____

_____ − _____ = _____

_____ − _____ = _____

5. Write the missing signs to finish the fact family.

9 ◯ 5 = 4   4 ◯ 5 = 9

5 ◯ 4 = 9   9 ◯ 4 = 5

6. Write the missing signs to finish the fact family.

11 ◯ 3 = 8   8 ◯ 3 = 11

3 ◯ 8 = 11   11 ◯ 8 = 3

Using Addition Facts to Subtract

Use addition and subtraction facts.

Write the missing numbers.

1. $9 - \boxed{4} = 5$

$\begin{array}{r} \boxed{4} \\ + \\ \hline 9 \end{array}$

2. $8 - \boxed{} = 3$

$\begin{array}{r} \boxed{} \\ + \\ \hline 8 \end{array}$

3. $11 - \boxed{} = 6$

$\begin{array}{r} \boxed{} \\ + \\ \hline 11 \end{array}$

4. $12 - \boxed{} = 4$

$\begin{array}{r} \boxed{} \\ + \\ \hline 12 \end{array}$

Write the answer.

5. Maya has 7 plums.

   She gives away 3 plums.

   How many plums does she have left?

   _____ plums

6. Emily has 10 stickers.

   She gives 3 stickers to Mark.

   How many stickers does she have left?

   _____ stickers

Choose an Operation

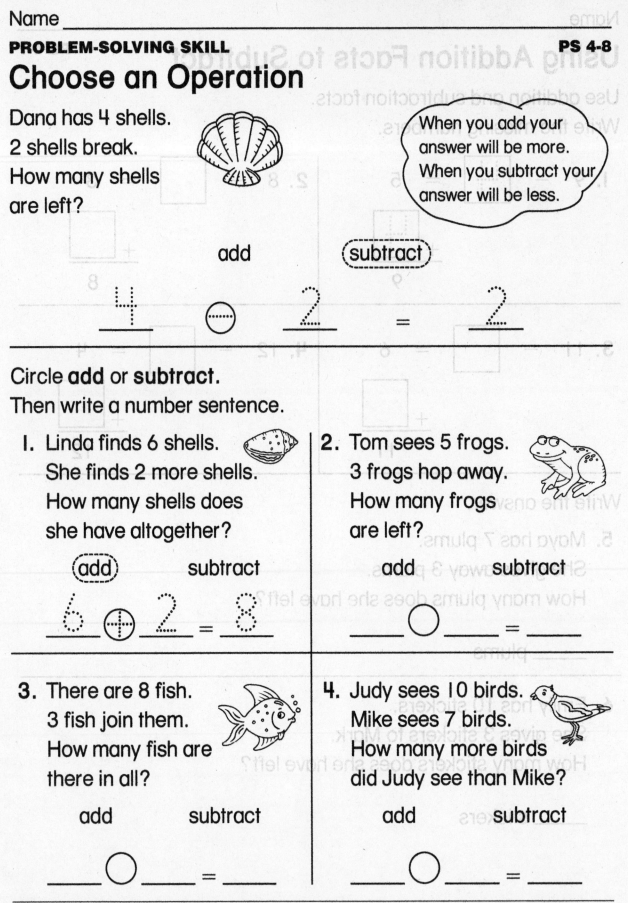

Dana has 4 shells.
2 shells break.
How many shells
are left?

When you add your
answer will be more.
When you subtract your
answer will be less.

add   (subtract)

4 ⊙ 2 = 2

Circle **add** or **subtract**.
Then write a number sentence.

1. Linda finds 6 shells.
She finds 2 more shells.
How many shells does
she have altogether?

(add)   subtract

6 ⊕ 2 = 8

2. Tom sees 5 frogs.
3 frogs hop away.
How many frogs
are left?

add   subtract

___ ◯ ___ = ___

---

3. There are 8 fish.
3 fish join them.
How many fish are
there in all?

add   subtract

___ ◯ ___ = ___

4. Judy sees 10 birds.
Mike sees 7 birds.
How many more birds
did Judy see than Mike?

add   subtract

___ ◯ ___ = ___

Using the page Encourage children to *look back* and *check* that their answer is less than the number they subtracted from or more than the numbers they added.

Name _____

Playful Puppies

Complete the number sentence.

Patty's dog had 9 puppies.

6 puppies are brown.

The rest are black.

How many puppies are black?

_9_ ⊖ _6_ = _3_

_3_ black puppies

Add to find how many in all. Subtract to find the difference.

Complete the number sentence.

1. There are 11 toys. The puppies chew up 2 toys.
   How many toys are left?

   _____ ◯ _____ = _____

   _____ toys left

2. 5 puppies nap on a mat. 4 puppies nap on a bed.
   How many puppies nap in all?

   _____ ◯ _____ = _____

   _____ puppies

   4 puppies wake up.
   How many puppies are still napping?

   _____ ◯ _____ = _____

   _____ puppies

Writing in Math

3. Write a subtraction story about puppies.
   Use pictures, numbers, or words.

Using the page Help children **plan** by talking with them about clues that help them to decide whether to add or subtract. Then have them **solve** the exercise.

Identifying Solid Figures

Finish drawing the toys.

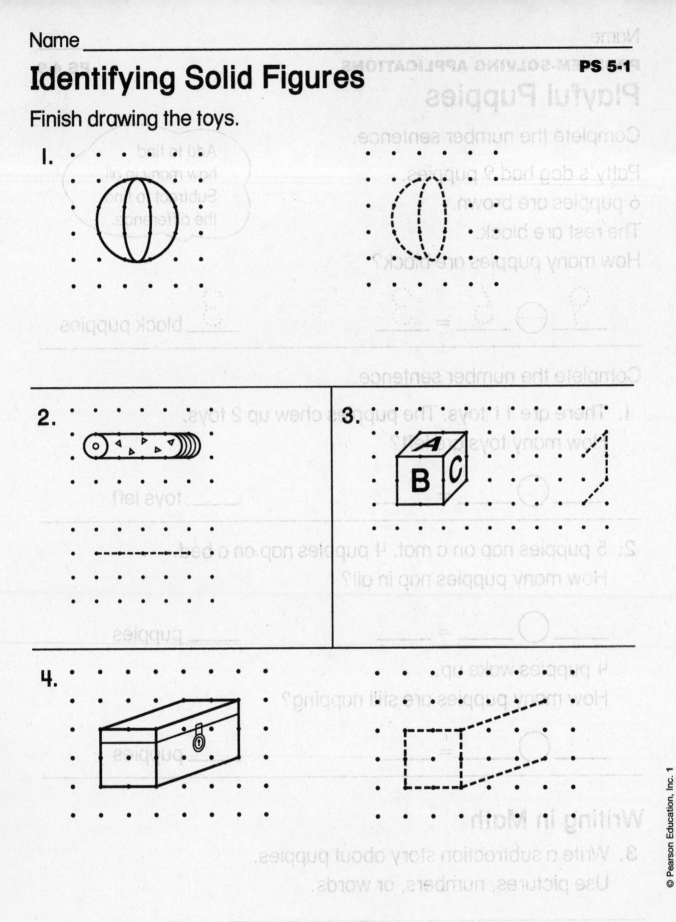

1.

2.

3.

4.

Flat Surfaces and Vertices

Draw a line from the clue to the solid figure.

1. Dana is going to the beach. She is taking an object with her that has 0 vertices and 0 flat surfaces. What solid figure does the object look like?

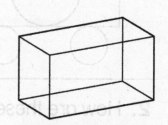

Cone

2. Shawn brought juice in an object that has 0 vertices and 2 flat surfaces. What solid figure does the object look like?

Cylinder

3. Carlos used clay to make a solid figure with 0 vertices and 1 flat surface. What solid figure did he make?

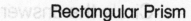

Rectangular Prism

4. The present Dan receives has 8 vertices and 6 flat faces. What solid does the present look like?

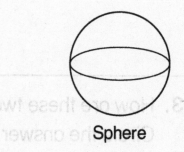

Sphere

Relating Plane Shapes to Solid Figures PS 5-3

1. Linda drew a circus train.
   She traced these solid figures
   to make the shapes for her train.
   Use the same color to color
   the part of the solid figure
   to match the shape she traced.

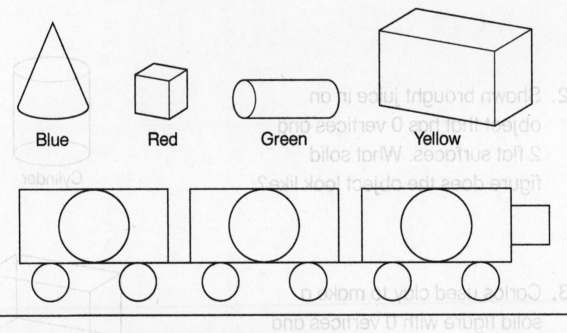

Blue   Red   Green   Yellow

2. How are these two clown hats alike?
   Circle the answer.

   same shape   same size

3. How are these two presents alike?
   Circle the answer.

   same shape   same size

Identifying Plane Shapes

Look at the pictures. Choose a name from the box below that names the plane shape that the picture shows. Write the name.

Triangle	Rectangle	Circle	Square

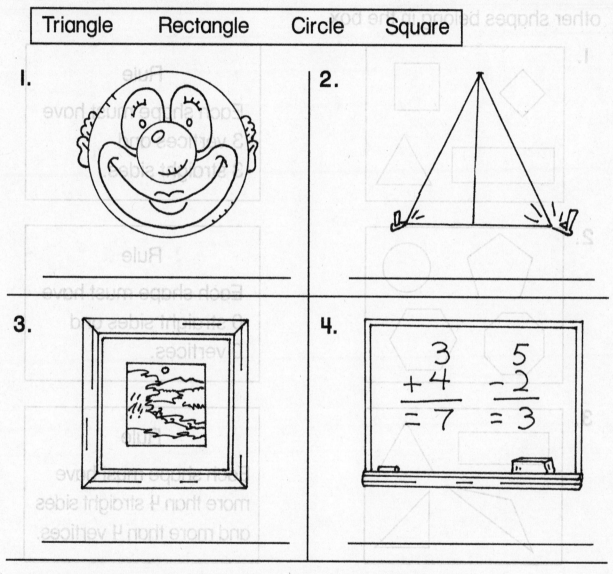

1. _____

2. _____

3. _____

4. _____

5. Draw the shape that comes next in the pattern.

_____

Properties of Plane Shapes

Cross out the shape in each box that
does not belong. Then draw a line
to the rule that tells why all of the
other shapes belong in the box.

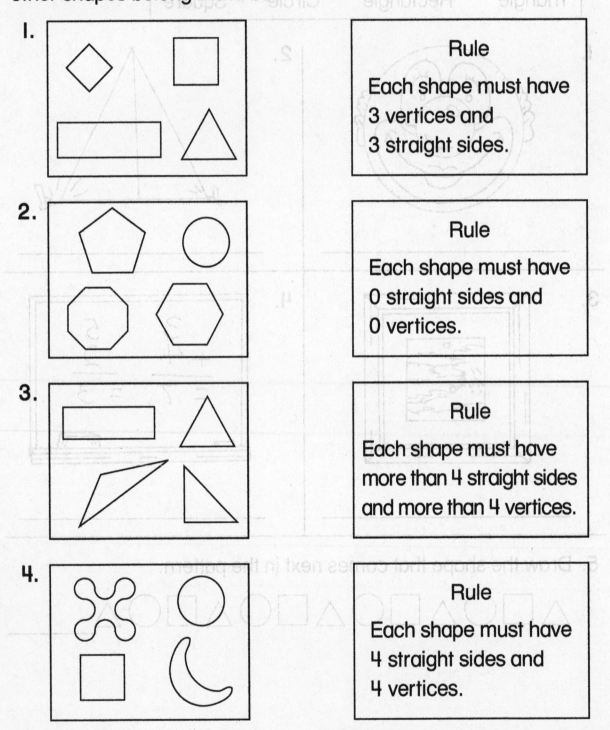

1.

Rule

Each shape must have
3 vertices and
3 straight sides.

2.

Rule

Each shape must have
0 straight sides and
0 vertices.

3.

Rule

Each shape must have
more than 4 straight sides
and more than 4 vertices.

4.

Rule

Each shape must have
4 straight sides and
4 vertices.

Same Size and Same Shape

Use the shapes in the house to follow the directions.

Directions

1. Find the squares that match.
   Color them blue.

2. Find the triangles that match.
   Color them red.

3. Find two other shapes that match.
   Color them green.

Symmetry

Which shapes can be folded so that both
parts match? Draw a line of symmetry to
show the fold lines.

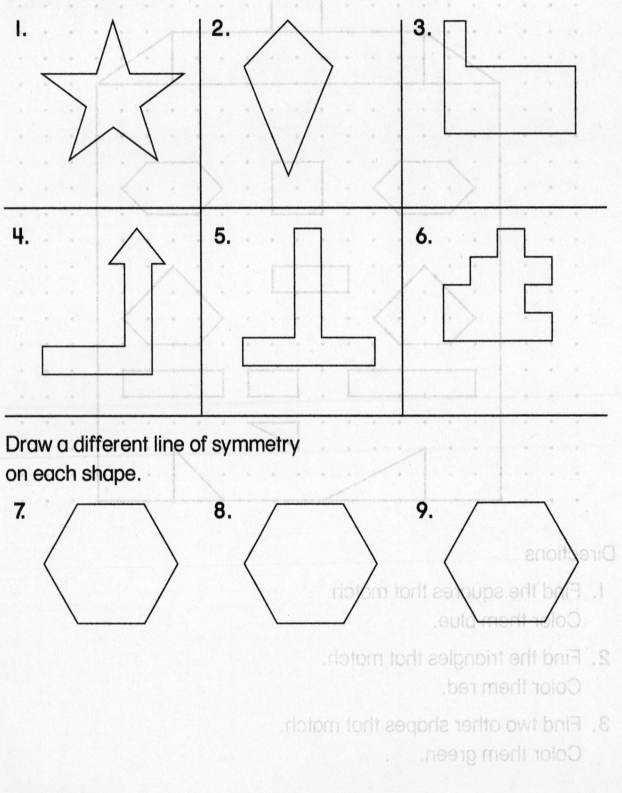

1.

2.

3.

4.

5.

6.

Draw a different line of symmetry
on each shape.

7.

8.

9.

Slides, Flips, and Turns

Help Gene put the missing piece in each puzzle.
Circle the way that he should move each shape to
make it fit.

1.

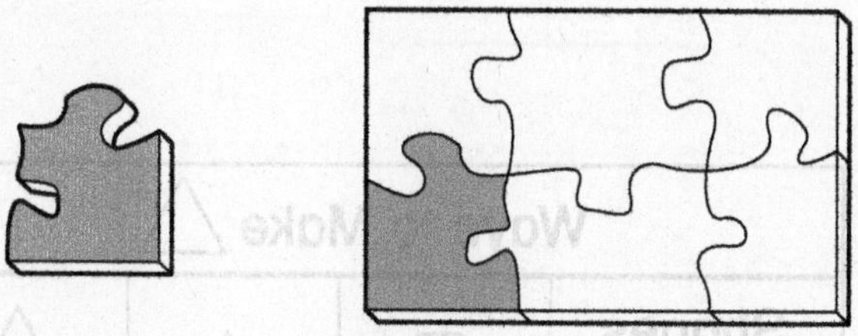

slide
flip
turn

2.

slide
flip
turn

3.

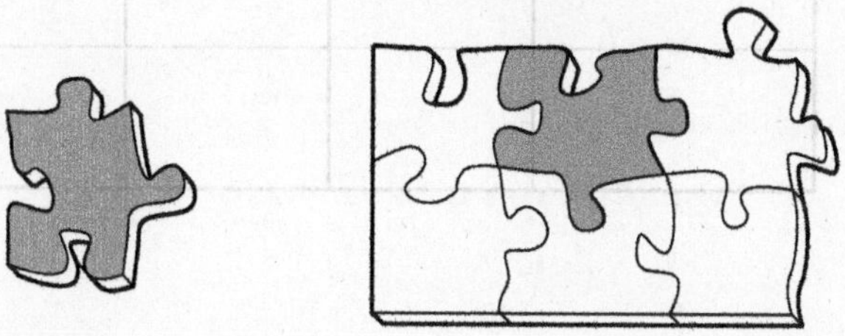

slide
flip
turn

4.

slide
flip
turn

5. Circle the shape that will fit if you turn it, or flip it, or slide it.

PROBLEM-SOLVING STRATEGY

Make an Organized List

How many ways can you make this shape?

Use pattern blocks.

Make a list to keep track.

Step 1: Decide which blocks
you can use.

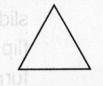

Step 2: Decide how many of
each block you need to
make the shape.

Ways to Make △			
Shapes I Used	⬤	△	◇
Way 1	1	1	0

Step 3: Try other shapes.
Fill in as many spaces
as you can.

There are _____ ways to make a shape the same size.

© Pearson Education, Inc. 1

Using the page Have children *look back* at their shapes by placing pattern blocks over the shape to *check* that the blocks make the same shape.

Equal Parts

Read each story. Circle the shape that
shows what Maya did.

1. Maya drew a flag.
   The flag had 4 equal parts.

2. Maya cut a cake into
   6 equal parts.

3. Maya planted flowers in
   the garden. She put different
   flowers in each of 8 equal parts.

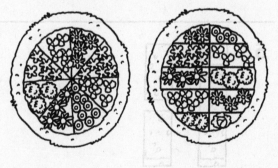

4. Help Maya divide this shape
   into 6 equal parts.
   Draw straight lines.

Halves

Lilly and Milly are twins. They will share lunch and a snack. Each will get $\frac{1}{2}$ of everything.

Circle the pair that shows halves.

1.

2.

3.

4.

5.

6.

7. Mary, Martha, and Kemba shared 1 cookie.
   Mary ate $\frac{1}{2}$ of the cookie.
   Kemba ate $\frac{1}{2}$ of the cookie.
   Was there any cookie left for Martha?

   _____

Thirds and Fourths

Color one part of each shape. Circle the fraction.

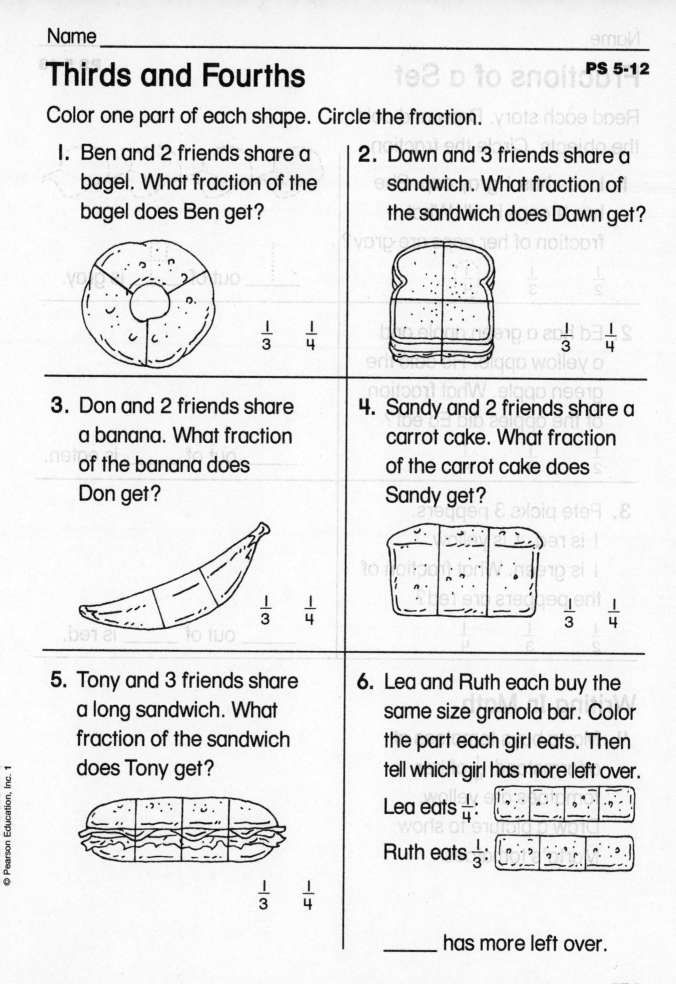

1. Ben and 2 friends share a bagel. What fraction of the bagel does Ben get?

$\frac{1}{3}$ $\frac{1}{4}$

2. Dawn and 3 friends share a sandwich. What fraction of the sandwich does Dawn get?

$\frac{1}{3}$ $\frac{1}{4}$

3. Don and 2 friends share a banana. What fraction of the banana does Don get?

$\frac{1}{3}$ $\frac{1}{4}$

4. Sandy and 2 friends share a carrot cake. What fraction of the carrot cake does Sandy get?

$\frac{1}{3}$ $\frac{1}{4}$

5. Tony and 3 friends share a long sandwich. What fraction of the sandwich does Tony get?

$\frac{1}{3}$ $\frac{1}{4}$

6. Lea and Ruth each buy the same size granola bar. Color the part each girl eats. Then tell which girl has more left over.

Lea eats $\frac{1}{4}$:

Ruth eats $\frac{1}{3}$:

_____ has more left over.

Name _____

Fractions of a Set

PS 5-13

Read each story. Draw and color the objects. Circle the fraction.

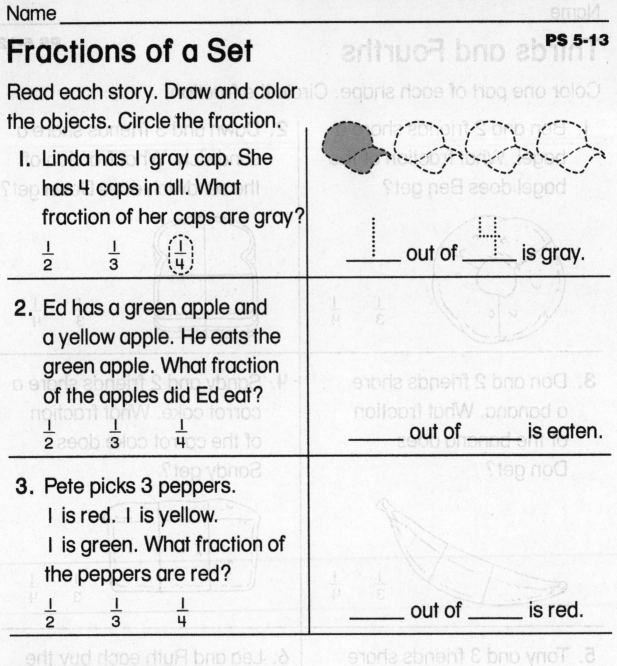

1. Linda has 1 gray cap. She has 4 caps in all. What fraction of her caps are gray?

   $\frac{1}{2}$ $\frac{1}{3}$ $\frac{1}{4}$

   ____ out of ____ is gray.

2. Ed has a green apple and a yellow apple. He eats the green apple. What fraction of the apples did Ed eat?

   $\frac{1}{2}$ $\frac{1}{3}$ $\frac{1}{4}$

   ____ out of ____ is eaten.

3. Pete picks 3 peppers. 1 is red. 1 is yellow. 1 is green. What fraction of the peppers are red?

   $\frac{1}{2}$ $\frac{1}{3}$ $\frac{1}{4}$

   ____ out of ____ is red.

Writing In Math

4. Marta buys tomatoes at a farmstand. $\frac{1}{4}$ of her tomatoes are yellow. Draw a picture to show Marta's tomatoes.

© Pearson Education, Inc. 1

60   Use with Lesson 5-13.

Non-Unit Fractions

Color the objects or the parts
to show the fraction.

1. $\frac{2}{4}$ of the beach umbrella
   is purple.

2. $\frac{2}{3}$ of the lobsters are red.

3. $\frac{3}{4}$ of the drinks are lemonade.

4. Color to show $\frac{3}{6}$ of the pizza.

5. Color to show $\frac{4}{6}$ of the cans.

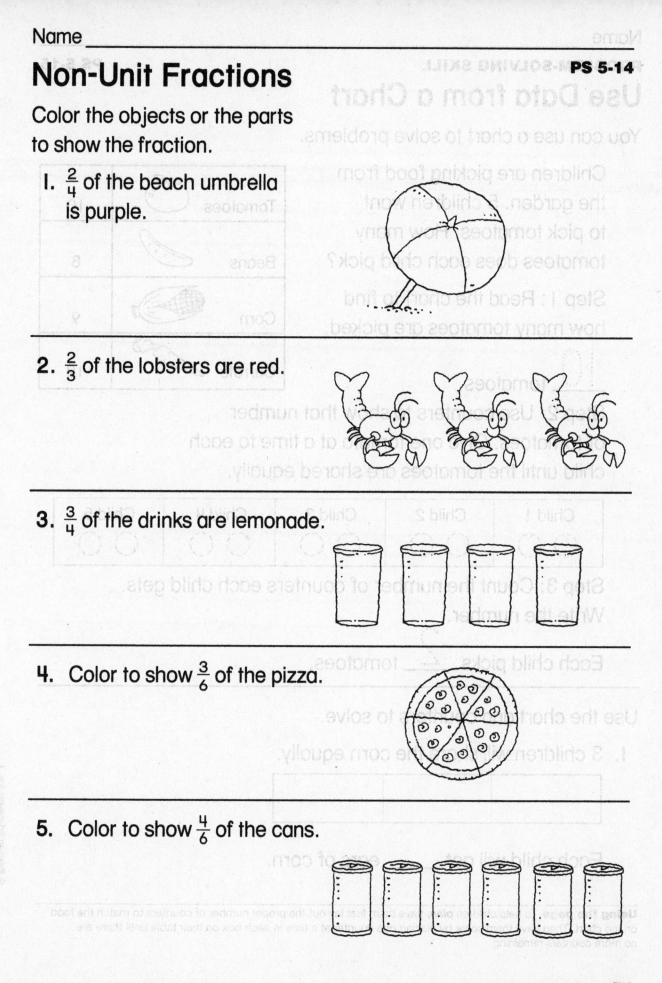

Name _____

PROBLEM-SOLVING SKILL

Use Data from a Chart

You can use a chart to solve problems.

Children are picking food from
the garden. 5 children want
to pick tomatoes. How many
tomatoes does each child pick?

Tomatoes	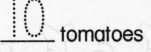	10
Beans		8
Corn		9
Carrots		12

Step 1: Read the chart to find
how many tomatoes are picked.

__10__ tomatoes

Step 2: Use counters to show that number
of tomatoes. Give one tomato at a time to each
child until the tomatoes are shared equally.

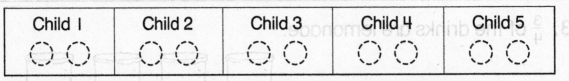

Child 1	Child 2	Child 3	Child 4	Child 5

Step 3: Count the number of counters each child gets.
Write the number.

Each child picks __2__ tomatoes.

Use the chart and counters to solve.

1. 3 children will share the corn equally.

Each child will get _____ ears of corn.

Using the page To help children *plan*, have them first lay out the proper number of counters to match the food
on the chart. Then have them *solve* by placing one counter at a time in each box on their table until there are
no more counters remaining.

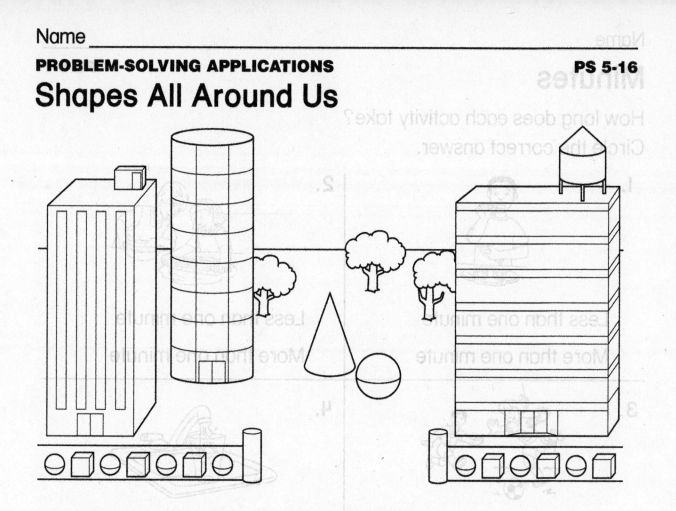

Shapes All Around Us

1. Color each sphere red. Write how many. _____

2. Color each rectangular prism blue. Write how many. _____

3. Color each cube yellow. Write how many. _____

4. Color each cone orange. Write how many. _____

5. Color each cylinder purple. Write the number. _____

6. Write a number sentence to tell how many more spheres there are than cylinders.

_____ – _____ = _____

_____ more spheres

Using the page As children *read* the directions, make certain they *understand* that the shapes can be different sizes and dimensions as long as they have the same characteristics of the shape.

Name _____

Minutes

How long does each activity take?
Circle the correct answer.

1.

Less than one minute

More than one minute

2.

Less than one minute

More than one minute

3.

Less than one minute

More than one minute

4.

Less than one minute

More than one minute

5.

Less than one minute

More than one minute

6.

Less than one minute

More than one minute

7. Draw a picture to show something
   that you can do in about
   the same time as it takes
   to tie your shoes.

Understanding the Hour and Minute Hands

Write the time that comes next. Then draw the hour hand and the minute hand to show each time.

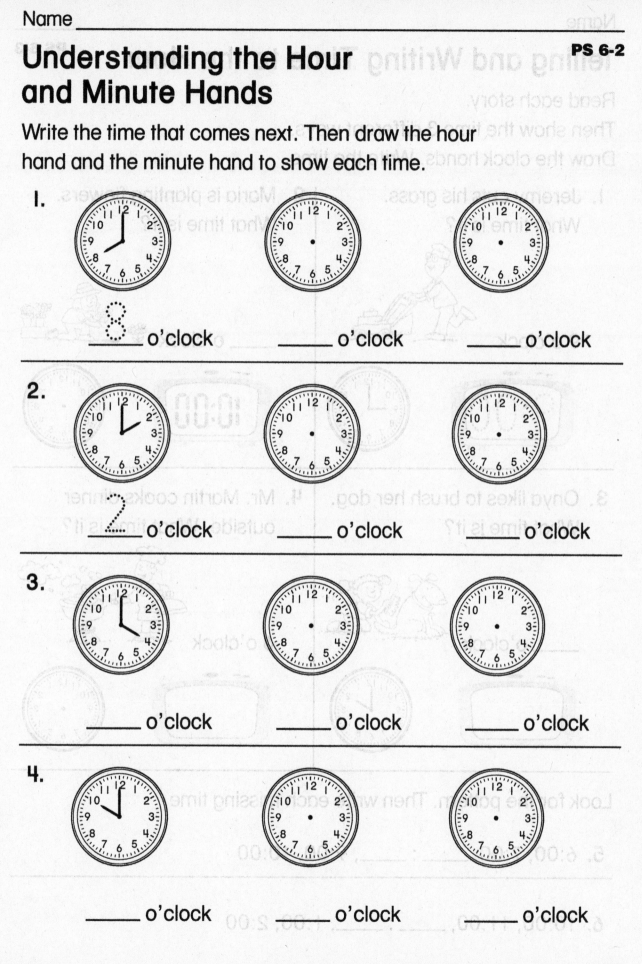

1.

_____ o'clock   _____ o'clock   _____ o'clock

2.

_____ o'clock   _____ o'clock   _____ o'clock

3.

_____ o'clock   _____ o'clock   _____ o'clock

4.

_____ o'clock   _____ o'clock   _____ o'clock

Telling and Writing Time to the Hour

Read each story.
Then show the time 3 different ways.
Draw the clock hands. Write the time.

1. Jeremy cuts his grass.
   What time is it?

   9 o'clock

2. Maria is planting flowers.
   What time is it?

   ____ o'clock

3. Onya likes to brush her dog.
   What time is it?

   ____ o'clock

4. Mr. Martin cooks dinner
   outside. What time is it?

   6 o'clock

Look for the pattern. Then write each missing time.

5. 6:00, 7:00, ____ : ____, 9:00, 10:00

6. 10:00, 11:00, ____ : ____, 1:00, 2:00

Telling and Writing Time to the Half Hour

Chip has to be home at 4 o'clock.
He stops every half hour to check the time.
Fill in the clock times that Chip sees.

Start ⟹

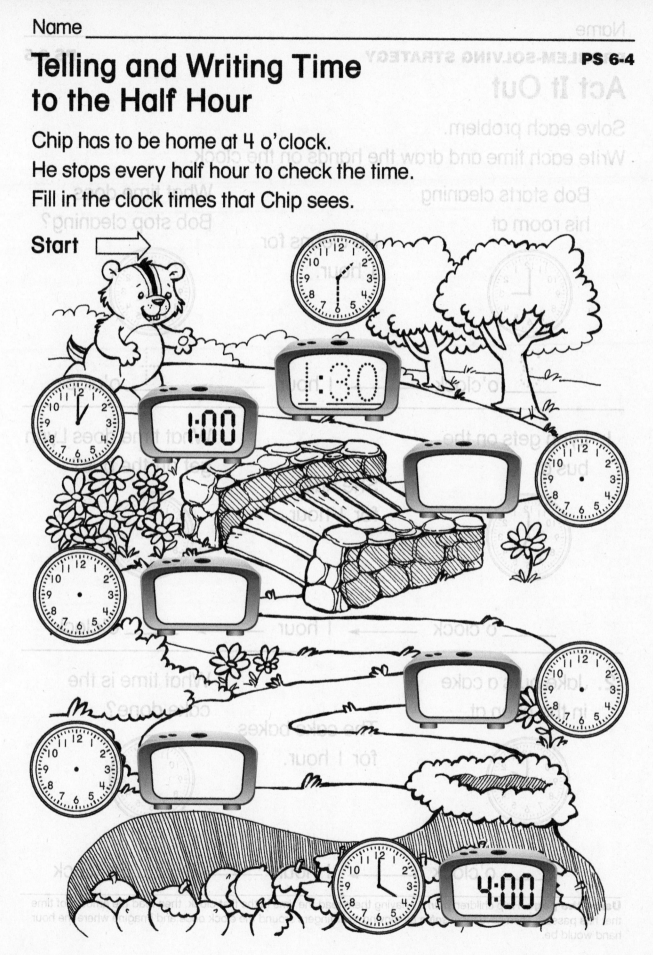

PROBLEM-SOLVING STRATEGY

Act It Out

Solve each problem.

Write each time and draw the hands on the clock.

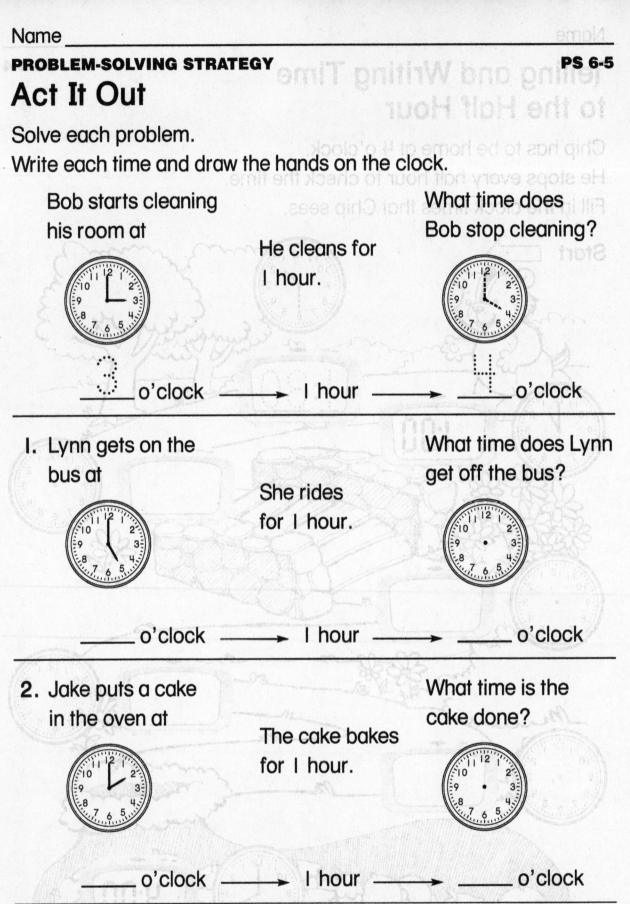

Bob starts cleaning
his room at

He cleans for
1 hour.

What time does
Bob stop cleaning?

_____ o'clock ——→ 1 hour ——→ _____ o'clock

1. Lynn gets on the
bus at

She rides
for 1 hour.

What time does Lynn
get off the bus?

_____ o'clock ——→ 1 hour ——→ _____ o'clock

2. Jake puts a cake
in the oven at

The cake bakes
for 1 hour.

What time is the
cake done?

_____ o'clock ——→ 1 hour ——→ _____ o'clock

Using the page Help children *plan* by having them read the time in the first clock, then read the amount of time that has passed. Then have them *solve* by moving their fingers around the clock once and imagine where the hour hand would be.

Ordering Events

Write 1, 2, and 3 to show the order in which
these events happen.

1.

_1_   _3_   _2_

2.

_____   _____   _____

3.

_____   _____   _____

4.

_____   _____   _____

Estimating Lengths of Time

Read the story.
Circle your answer.

1. Becky wants to practice her numbers. About how long will she count?

    about 1 minute   about 1 hour   about 1 day

2. The boys play checkers. About how long will they play?

    about 1 minute   about 1 hour   about 1 day

3. Misha walks her dog. About how long will that take?

    about 10 minutes   about 10 hours   about 10 days

Write your answer.

4. Mom makes dinner. Does it take about 1 minute or about 1 hour?

    about _____

5. Dad is building a tree house. Will it take about 1 hour or about 1 day?

    about _____

Use Data from a Schedule

This movie schedule shows the names of the movies and the time each movie starts.

Movie Schedule	
Time	**Movie**
1:00	Dinosaurs and Dragons
2:30	Pokey the Pony
4:00	Haunted Hill
5:30	Volcano!

Use the schedule to answer the questions.

1. What time does Dinosaurs and Dragons start? _____

2. Circle the movie that starts at the time shown on the clock.

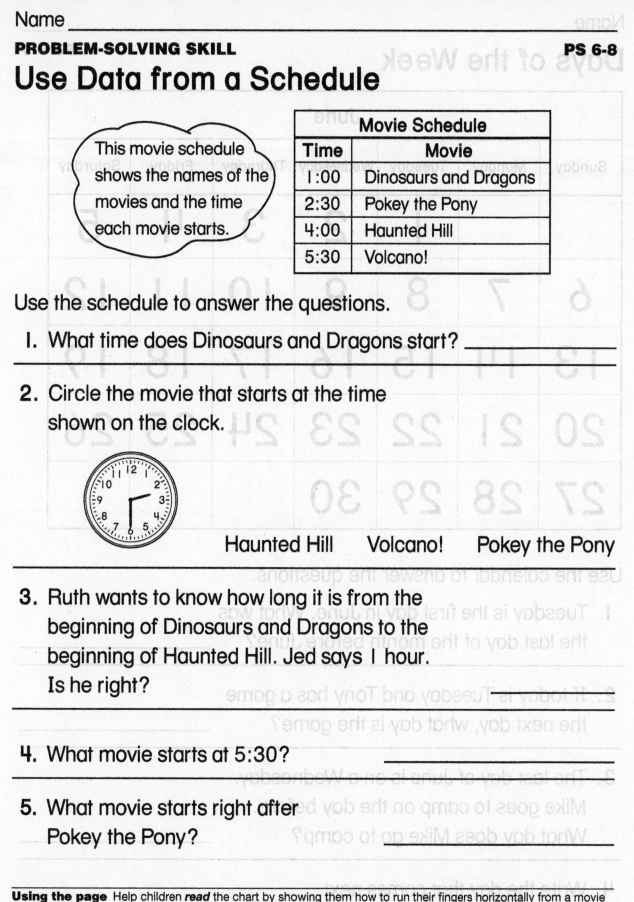

   Haunted Hill   Volcano!   Pokey the Pony

3. Ruth wants to know how long it is from the beginning of Dinosaurs and Dragons to the beginning of Haunted Hill. Jed says 1 hour. Is he right?
_____

4. What movie starts at 5:30? _____

5. What movie starts right after Pokey the Pony? _____

Using the page Help children **read** the chart by showing them how to run their fingers horizontally from a movie title to the time it begins. You may even suggest that they hold a straight edge beneath them. This technique will help children **understand** how to answer time-related questions.

Days of the Week

June						
Sunday	Monday	Tuesday	Wednesday	Thursday	Friday	Saturday
		1	2	3	4	5
6	7	8	9	10	11	12
13	14	15	16	17	18	19
20	21	22	23	24	25	26
27	28	29	30			

Use the calendar to answer the questions.

1. Tuesday is the first day in June. What was
   the last day of the month before June? _____

2. If today is Tuesday and Tony has a game
   the next day, what day is the game? _____

3. The last day of June is on a Wednesday.
   Mike goes to camp on the day before.
   What day does Mike go to camp? _____

4. Write the day that comes next.
   Thursday, Friday, Saturday, _____

Months of the Year

| January | February | March | April |

January
S	M	T	W	T	F	S
				1	2	3
4	5	6	7	8	9	10
11	12	13	14	15	16	17
18	19	20	21	22	23	24
25	26	27	28	29	30	31

February
S	M	T	W	T	F	S
1	2	3	4	5	6	7
8	9	10	11	12	13	14
15	16	17	18	19	20	21
22	23	24	25	26	27	28

March
S	M	T	W	T	F	S
1	2	3	4	5	6	7
8	9	10	11	12	13	14
15	16	17	18	19	20	21
22	23	24	25	26	27	28
29	30	31				

April
S	M	T	W	T	F	S
				1	2	3	4
5	6	7	8	9	10	11
12	13	14	15	16	17	18
19	20	21	22	23	24	25
26	27	28	29	30		

May
S	M	T	W	T	F	S
					1	2
3	4	5	6	7	8	9
10	11	12	13	14	15	16
17	18	19	20	21	22	23
24/31	25	26	27	28	29	30

June
S	M	T	W	T	F	S
	1	2	3	4	5	6
7	8	9	10	11	12	13
14	15	16	17	18	19	20
21	22	23	24	25	26	27
28	29	30				

July
S	M	T	W	T	F	S
				1	2	3	4
5	6	7	8	9	10	11
12	13	14	15	16	17	18
19	20	21	22	23	24	25
26	27	28	29	30	31	

August
S	M	T	W	T	F	S
						1
2	3	4	5	6	7	8
9	10	11	12	13	14	15
16	17	18	19	20	21	22
23/30	24/31	25	26	27	28	29

September
S	M	T	W	T	F	S
		1	2	3	4	5
6	7	8	9	10	11	12
13	14	15	16	17	18	19
20	21	22	23	24	25	26
27	28	29	30			

October
S	M	T	W	T	F	S
					1	2	3
4	5	6	7	8	9	10
11	12	13	14	15	16	17
18	19	20	21	22	23	24
25	26	27	28	29	30	31

November
S	M	T	W	T	F	S
1	2	3	4	5	6	7
8	9	10	11	12	13	14
15	16	17	18	19	20	21
22	23	24	25	26	27	28
29	30					

December
S	M	T	W	T	F	S
		1	2	3	4	5
6	7	8	9	10	11	12
13	14	15	16	17	18	19
20	21	22	23	24	25	26
27	28	29	30	31		

Use the calendar to answer the questions.

1. Mike's birthday is in the third month of the year. What month is that? _____

2. The last month of the year is Karen's favorite month. What month is that? _____

3. Kevin visits his Grandma the month after July. What month is that? _____

4. Thanksgiving Day is in November. What month comes before November? _____

5. What is another way to write each date? Draw a line to match the dates.

May 10, 2005   9/3/2005

September 3, 2005   5/10/2005

PROBLEM-SOLVING APPLICATIONS PS 6-11

What's Inside the Egg?

1. Larry has a block with pictures of animals
   that live in a pond. What shape is the block?

   _____

2. Larry sees 8 animals at the pond.
   5 animals are in the water.
   How many animals are not in the water?

   _____ − _____ = _____

3. At 11:30 Larry sees a beaver at the pond.
   Show the time on both clocks.

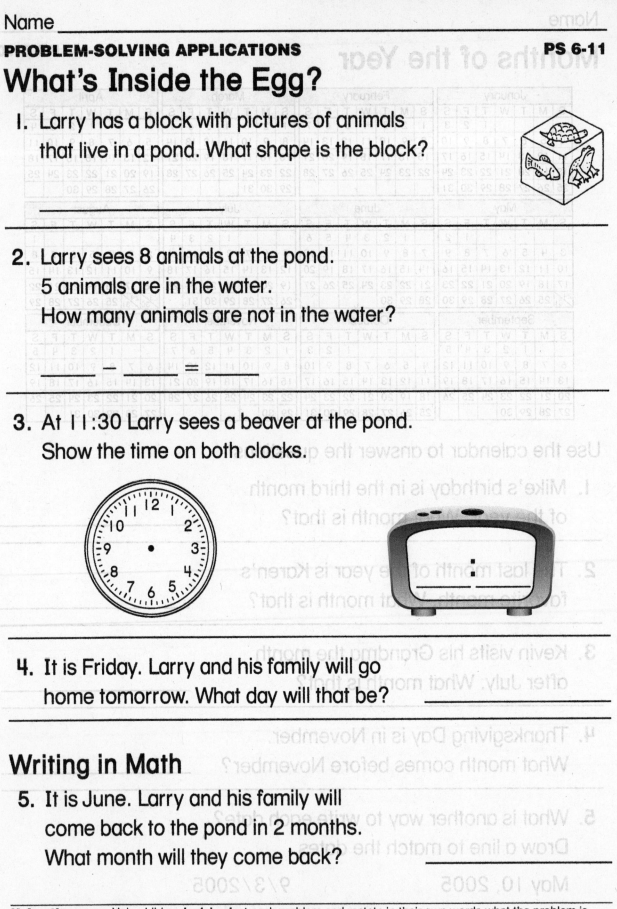

4. It is Friday. Larry and his family will go
   home tomorrow. What day will that be? _____

Writing in Math

5. It is June. Larry and his family will
   come back to the pond in 2 months.
   What month will they come back? _____

Using the page Help children *look back* at each problem and restate in their own words what the problem is asking. Then have them *check* that their solutions answer that question.

74 Use with Lesson 6-11.

Numbers to 19

Read each story.
Write the missing numbers.

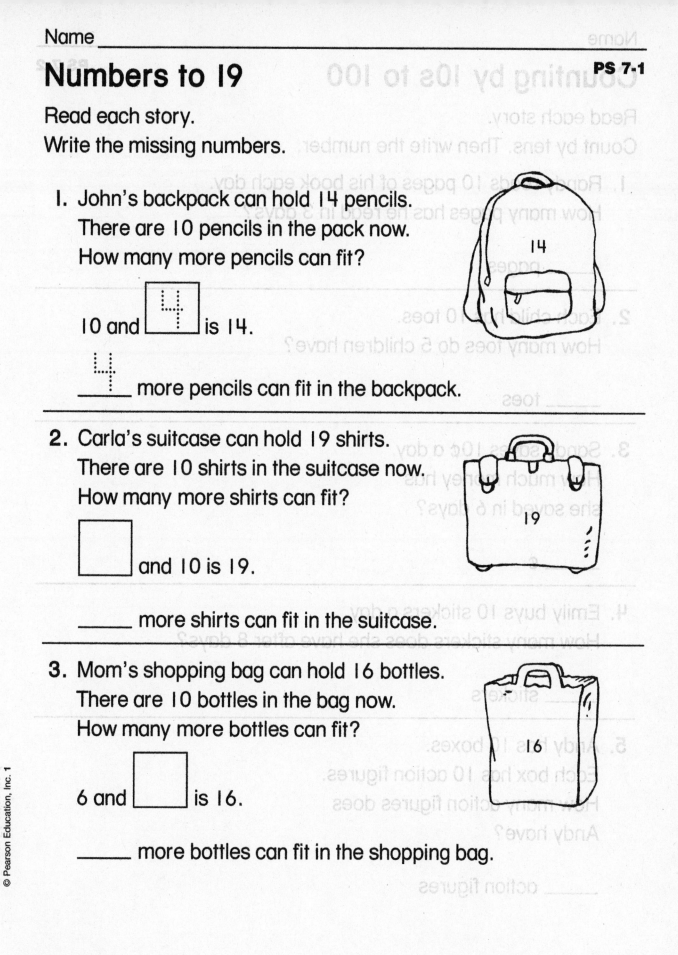

1. John's backpack can hold 14 pencils.
   There are 10 pencils in the pack now.
   How many more pencils can fit?

   10 and ⌐4⌐ is 14.

   ⌐4⌐ more pencils can fit in the backpack.

2. Carla's suitcase can hold 19 shirts.
   There are 10 shirts in the suitcase now.
   How many more shirts can fit?

   [ ] and 10 is 19.

   _____ more shirts can fit in the suitcase.

3. Mom's shopping bag can hold 16 bottles.
   There are 10 bottles in the bag now.
   How many more bottles can fit?

   6 and [ ] is 16.

   _____ more bottles can fit in the shopping bag.

Counting by 10s to 100

Read each story.

Count by tens. Then write the number.

1. Randy reads 10 pages of his book each day.
   How many pages has he read in 3 days?

   _____ pages

2. Each child has 10 toes.
   How many toes do 5 children have?

   _____ toes

3. Sandy saves 10¢ a day.
   How much money has
   she saved in 6 days?

   _____ ¢

4. Emily buys 10 stickers a day.
   How many stickers does she have after 8 days?

   _____ stickers

5. Andy has 10 boxes.
   Each box has 10 action figures.
   How many action figures does
   Andy have?

   _____ action figures

Hundred Chart

Look at these parts of the hundred chart.
Write the missing numbers.

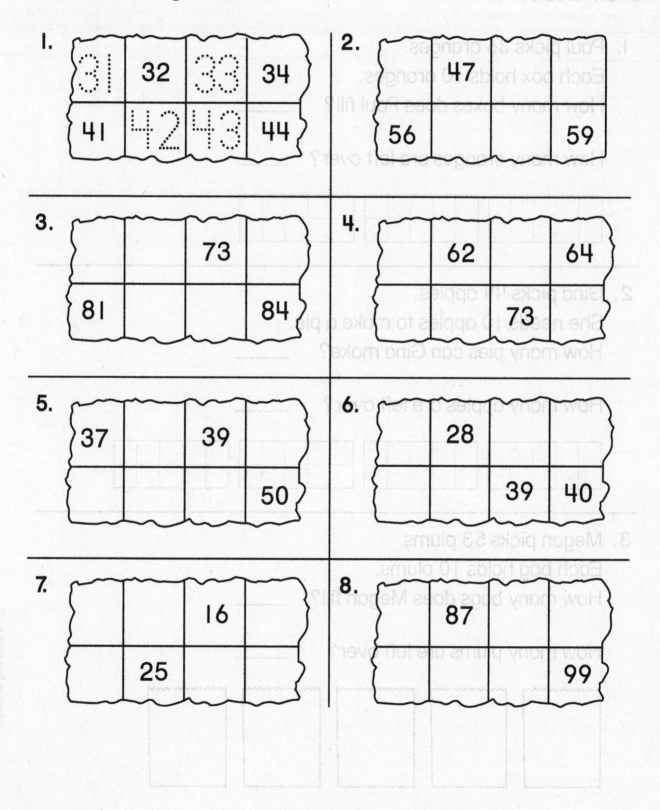

1.

31	32	33	34
41	42	43	44

2.

	47		
56			59

3.

		73	
81			84

4.

	62		64
		73	

5.

37		39	
			50

6.

	28		
		39	40

7.

		16	
	25		

8.

	87		
			99

Counting with Groups of 10 and Leftovers

Draw to solve.

1. Paul picks 36 oranges.
   Each box holds 10 oranges.
   How many boxes does Paul fill? _____

   How many oranges are left over? _____

2. Gina picks 44 apples.
   She needs 10 apples to make a pie.
   How many pies can Gina make? _____

   How many apples are left over? _____

3. Megan picks 53 plums.
   Each bag holds 10 plums.
   How many bags does Megan fill? _____

   How many plums are left over? _____

Name _____

Estimating with Groups of 10

Circle all of the numbers that answer the question.

1. Raul estimates that he saw about 40 robins in the park. Which numbers could show how many robins Raul really saw?

   13   28   32   38   42   48

2. Kit estimates that she put about 60 pennies in her penny bank. Which numbers could show how many pennies Kit really put in her bank?

   29   43   52   58   63   67

3. Jonah estimates that there are about 80 pieces in the jigsaw puzzle he is working on. Which numbers could show how many puzzle pieces there really are?

   58   67   72   79   83   92

4. Linda estimates that she collected about 30 stickers this month. Which numbers could show how many stickers Linda really collected?

   17   21   24   29   32   40

5. Rodrigo estimates that there are about 50 pictures in his photo album. Which numbers could show how many pictures he really has?

   29   35   42   47   51   55

PROBLEM-SOLVING SKILL

Use Data from a Graph

Tim started this graph to show his model collection.

He found 10 more model cars. Help him finish his graph.

Then answer the questions.

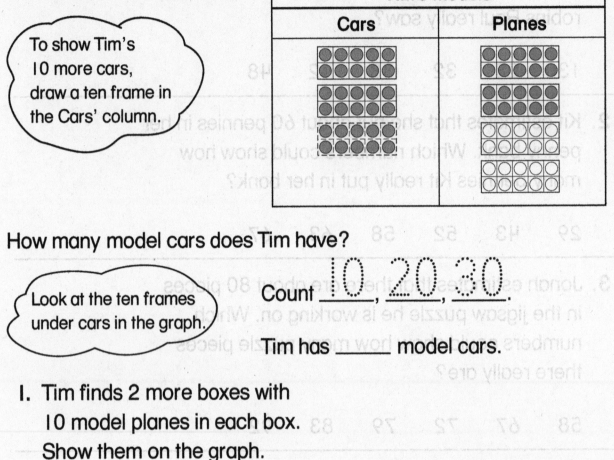

To show Tim's
10 more cars,
draw a ten frame in
the Cars' column.

How many model cars does Tim have?

Look at the ten frames
under cars in the graph.

Count ___10___, ___20___, ___30___.

Tim has _____ model cars.

1. Tim finds 2 more boxes with
   10 model planes in each box.
   Show them on the graph.

_____

2. How many model planes does Tim have? _____ model planes

Writing in Math

3. Write your own question about the graph.

_____

© Pearson Education, Inc. 1

Using the page *Read* the problem with the children. Help them *understand* that they must first complete the graph before they can answer the questions.

Skip-Counting Patterns on the Hundred Chart

Circle the numbers you say when you count by fives.
Put a box around the numbers you say when you count by twos.

| 21 | 22 | 23 | 24 | 25 | 26 | 27 | 28 | 29 | 30 |
| 31 | 32 | 33 | 34 | 35 | 36 | 37 | 38 | 39 | 40 |

Read each story.
Use this chart to help you answer the questions.

1. Dave packs newspapers in bundles of five.
   He has packed 5 bundles of newspapers.
   He packs 3 more bundles of newspapers.
   How many newspapers has Dave packed?

   _____ newspapers

2. Carlos collects 2 pencils from each student.
   He has 28 pencils.
   He collects pencils from 4 more students.
   How many pencils does he have now?

   _____ pencils

3. Marta feeds the fish every 3 days.
   Marta feeds the fish on June 3.
   Will she feed them on June 27?

   _____

June						
S	M	T	W	T	F	S
1	2	3	4	5	6	7
8	9	10	11	12	13	14
15	16	17	18	19	20	21
22	23	24	25	26	27	28
29	30					

Using Skip Counting

The fruit stand just opened. How many
of each kind of fruit is for sale?
Write the number you will skip count by.
Write how many in all.

Apples

Bananas

Pears

1. How many apples are for sale?

   Skip count by _____.   _____ apples in all

2. How many bananas are for sale?

   Skip count by _____.   _____ bananas in all

3. How many pears are for sale?

   Skip count by _____.   _____ pears in all

Find the pattern. Write the missing numbers.

4. 20, _____, 40, 50, _____, _____, 80, _____, 100

5. 25, _____, 35, 40, _____, _____, 55, _____, 65

6. 20, 18, 16, _____, 12, 10, _____, _____, 4, 2

Name _____

Look for a Pattern

Find a pattern. Then write the number.

1. Jan has 6 flower pots.
   She plants 4 flowers in each pot.
   How many flowers does she plant in all?

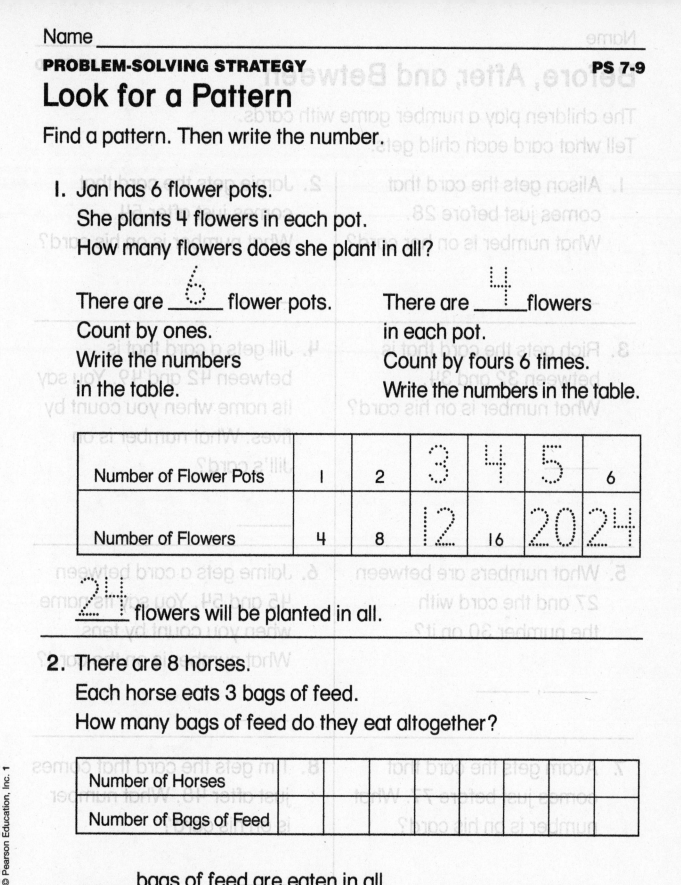

There are ___6___ flower pots.
Count by ones.
Write the numbers
in the table.

There are ___4___ flowers
in each pot.
Count by fours 6 times.
Write the numbers in the table.

Number of Flower Pots	1	2	3	4	5	6
Number of Flowers	4	8	12	16	20	24

___24___ flowers will be planted in all.

2. There are 8 horses.
   Each horse eats 3 bags of feed.
   How many bags of feed do they eat altogether?

Number of Horses								
Number of Bags of Feed								

_____ bags of feed are eaten in all.

Using the page Have children *look back* at the first number in each problem. Then have them *check* that they have written numbers in that many boxes on their tables.

Before, After, and Between

The children play a number game with cards.
Tell what card each child gets.

1. Alison gets the card that comes just before 28. What number is on her card?

   _____

2. Jamie gets the card that comes just after 54. What number is on his card?

3. Rich gets the card that is between 32 and 34. What number is on his card?

   _____

4. Jill gets a card that is between 42 and 49. You say its name when you count by fives. What number is on Jill's card?

   _____

5. What numbers are between 27 and the card with the number 30 on it?

   _____, _____

6. Jaime gets a card between 45 and 54. You say its name when you count by tens. What number is on the card?

   _____

7. Adam gets the card that comes just before 77. What number is on his card?

   _____

8. Tim gets the card that comes just after 48. What number is on his card?

   _____

Odd and Even Numbers

Draw the decorations from Betsy's garden party
to show each number. Try to make equal rows.
Circle **odd** or **even**.

1. 9 stars

odd

even

2. 12 moons

odd

even

3. 15 suns

odd

even

4. Betsy finds 4 more stars.
Does she have an odd or an
even number of stars now?

_____

5. Betsy breaks 3 suns. Does
she have an odd or an
even number of suns left?

_____

6. Here is a portion of the hundred chart.
Find the pattern. Write **even** or **odd**
to complete each sentence.

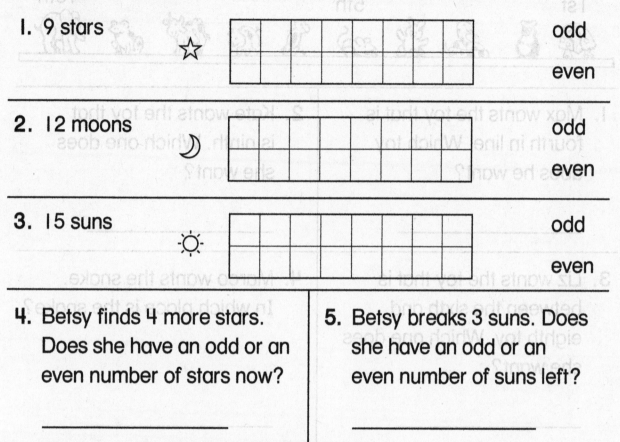

The numbers in circles are _____.

The numbers in squares are _____.

Ordinal Numbers Through Twentieth   **PS 7-12**

Help the salesperson in the toy store.

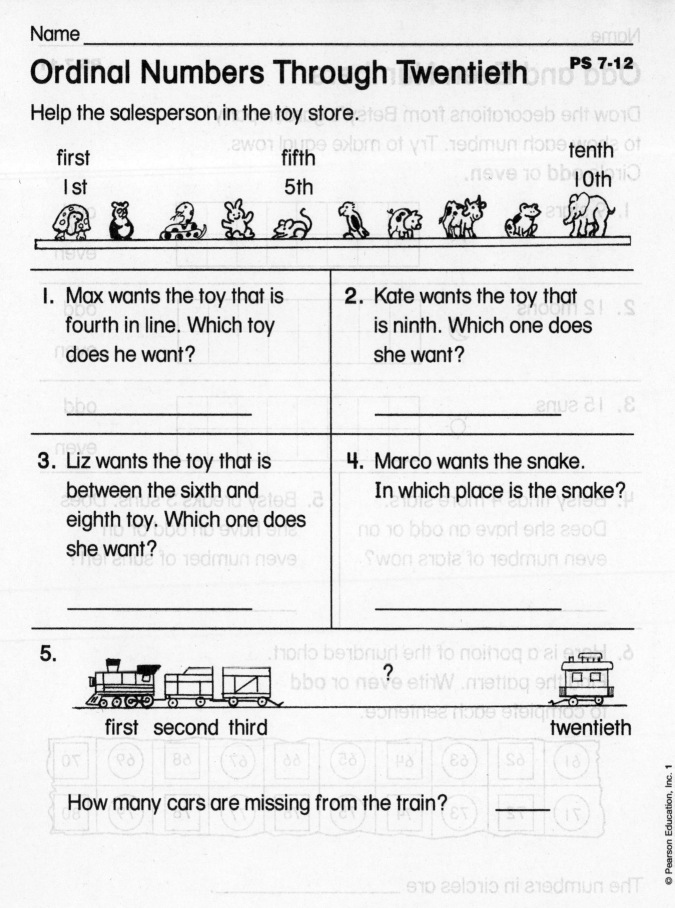

first   fifth   tenth

1st   5th   10th

1. Max wants the toy that is fourth in line. Which toy does he want?

   _____

2. Kate wants the toy that is ninth. Which one does she want?

   _____

3. Liz wants the toy that is between the sixth and eighth toy. Which one does she want?

   _____

4. Marco wants the snake. In which place is the snake?

   _____

5.

first second third   ?   twentieth

How many cars are missing from the train? _____

Name _____

By the Sea

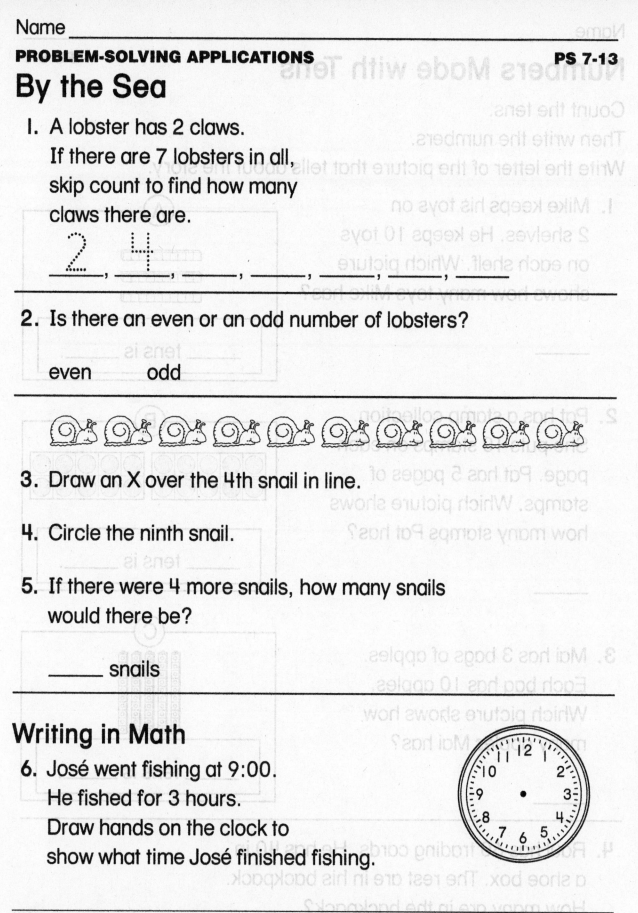

1. A lobster has 2 claws.
   If there are 7 lobsters in all,
   skip count to find how many
   claws there are.

   2 , 4 , _____ , _____ , _____ , _____ , _____

2. Is there an even or an odd number of lobsters?

   even   odd

3. Draw an X over the 4th snail in line.

4. Circle the ninth snail.

5. If there were 4 more snails, how many snails
   would there be?

   _____ snails

Writing in Math

6. José went fishing at 9:00.
   He fished for 3 hours.
   Draw hands on the clock to
   show what time José finished fishing.

© Pearson Education, Inc. 1

Using the page Help children *plan* by having them restate the question that is asked in each exercise. Then have them tell what they need to know to *solve* the exercise.

Numbers Made with Tens

Count the tens.

Then write the numbers.

Write the letter of the picture that tells about the story.

1. Mike keeps his toys on
   2 shelves. He keeps 10 toys
   on each shelf. Which picture
   shows how many toys Mike has?

   _____

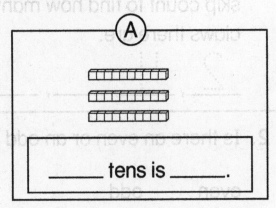

_____ tens is _____.

2. Pat has a stamp collection.
   She puts 10 stamps on each
   page. Pat has 5 pages of
   stamps. Which picture shows
   how many stamps Pat has?

   _____

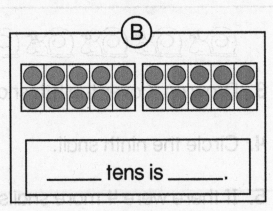

_____ tens is _____.

3. Mai has 3 bags of apples.
   Each bag has 10 apples.
   Which picture shows how
   many apples Mai has?

   _____

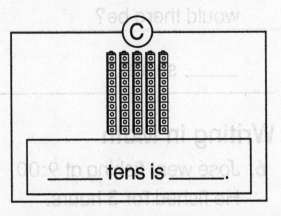

_____ tens is _____.

4. Raul has 60 trading cards. He has 40 in
   a shoe box. The rest are in his backpack.
   How many are in the backpack? _____

Tens and Ones

The children get points for the work they do in class.

They get a 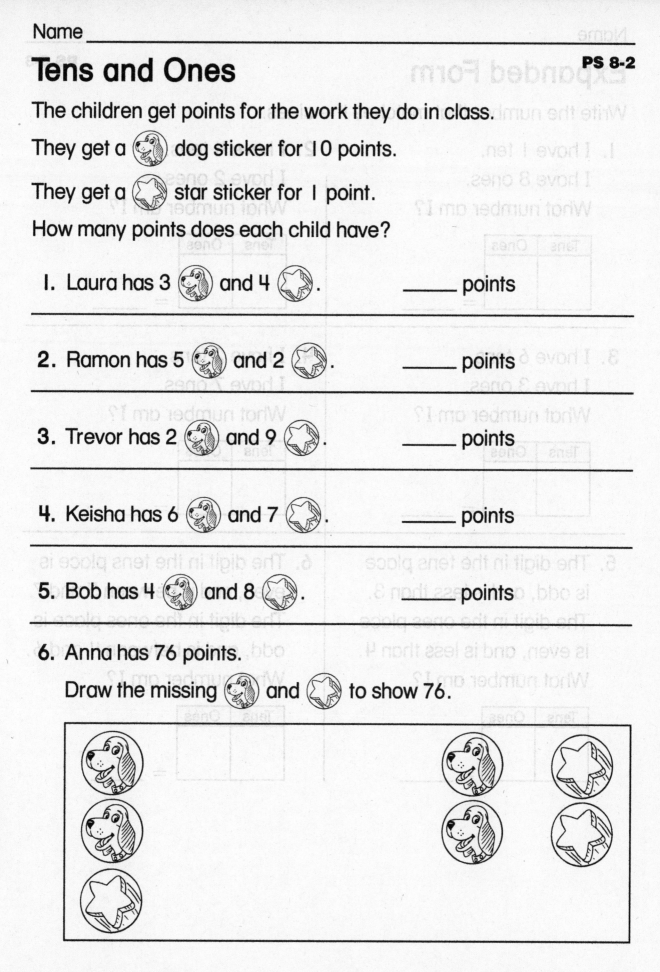 dog sticker for 10 points.

They get a ⭐ star sticker for 1 point.

How many points does each child have?

1. Laura has 3 🐕 and 4 ⭐ . _____ points

2. Ramon has 5 🐕 and 2 ⭐ . _____ points

3. Trevor has 2 🐕 and 9 ⭐ . _____ points

4. Keisha has 6 🐕 and 7 ⭐ . _____ points

5. Bob has 4 🐕 and 8 ⭐ . _____ points

6. Anna has 76 points.

   Draw the missing 🐕 and ⭐ to show 76.

Expanded Form

Write the number that matches the clues.

1. I have 1 ten.
I have 8 ones.
What number am I?

Tens	Ones

= _____

2. I have 4 tens.
I have 2 ones.
What number am I?

Tens	Ones

= _____

3. I have 6 tens.
I have 3 ones.
What number am I?

Tens	Ones

= _____

4. I have 2 tens.
I have 7 ones.
What number am I?

Tens	Ones

= _____

5. The digit in the tens place
is odd, and is less than 3.
The digit in the ones place
is even, and is less than 4.
What number am I?

Tens	Ones

= _____

6. The digit in the tens place is
even, and is between 5 and 7.
The digit in the ones place is
odd, and is between 4 and 6.
What number am I?

Tens	Ones

= _____

Ways to Make Numbers

How many more cubes do you need to make the
number in the circle? Write how many more tens
and how many more ones.

1. (24)

More

Tens	Ones

2. (31)

More

Tens	Ones

3. (47)

More

Tens	Ones

4. (60)

More

Tens	Ones

5. Use cubes to solve. Circle **yes** or **no**.

On Max's workmat there are 3 tens and 12 ones.
On Sam's workmat there are 4 tens and 2 ones.
Are the boys showing the same number on each
of their workmats?

yes   no

PROBLEM-SOLVING STRATEGY

Use Objects

Nina collects rocks. She finds 13 rocks at the beach.
She finds 26 rocks in the mountains. How many rocks
did Nina find?

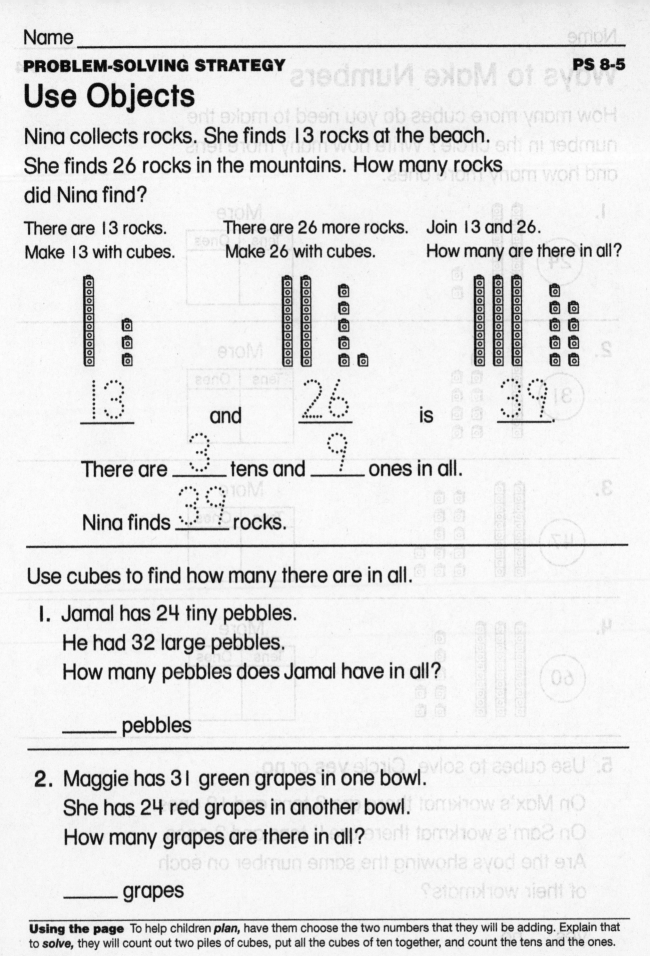

There are 13 rocks.   There are 26 more rocks.   Join 13 and 26.
Make 13 with cubes.   Make 26 with cubes.   How many are there in all?

13 and 26 is 39.

There are ___3___ tens and ___9___ ones in all.

Nina finds ___39___ rocks.

Use cubes to find how many there are in all.

1. Jamal has 24 tiny pebbles.
   He had 32 large pebbles.
   How many pebbles does Jamal have in all?

   _____ pebbles

2. Maggie has 31 green grapes in one bowl.
   She has 24 red grapes in another bowl.
   How many grapes are there in all?

   _____ grapes

Using the page To help children *plan,* have them choose the two numbers that they will be adding. Explain that to *solve,* they will count out two piles of cubes, put all the cubes of ten together, and count the tens and the ones.

1 More, 1 Less; 10 More, 10 Less

The children on the basketball team have team shirts.
Use the clues to find the number on each shirt.
Write the number.

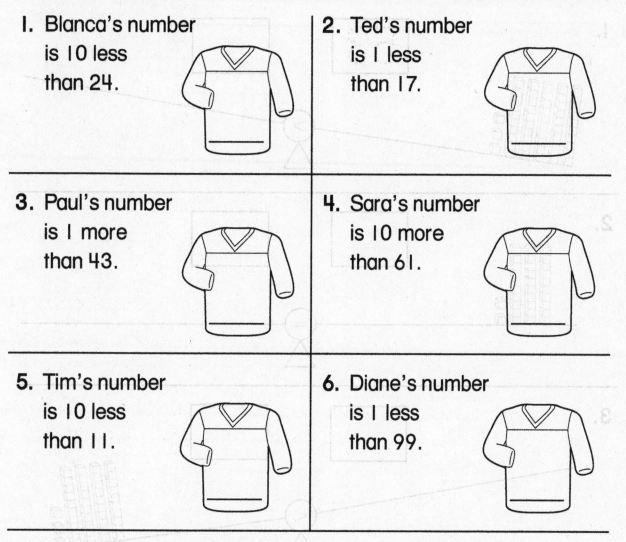

1. Blanca's number is 10 less than 24.

2. Ted's number is 1 less than 17.

3. Paul's number is 1 more than 43.

4. Sara's number is 10 more than 61.

5. Tim's number is 10 less than 11.

6. Diane's number is 1 less than 99.

7. Use the clues to write the number of each girl's shirt.

Kora's shirt number is 10 less than Marie's.
Marie's shirt number is 1 more than Peg's.
Peg's shirt number is 36.

_____   _____   _____
Kora   Marie   Peg

Comparing Numbers:
Greater Than, Less Than, Equal

Draw models to make each example true.
Write the numbers.

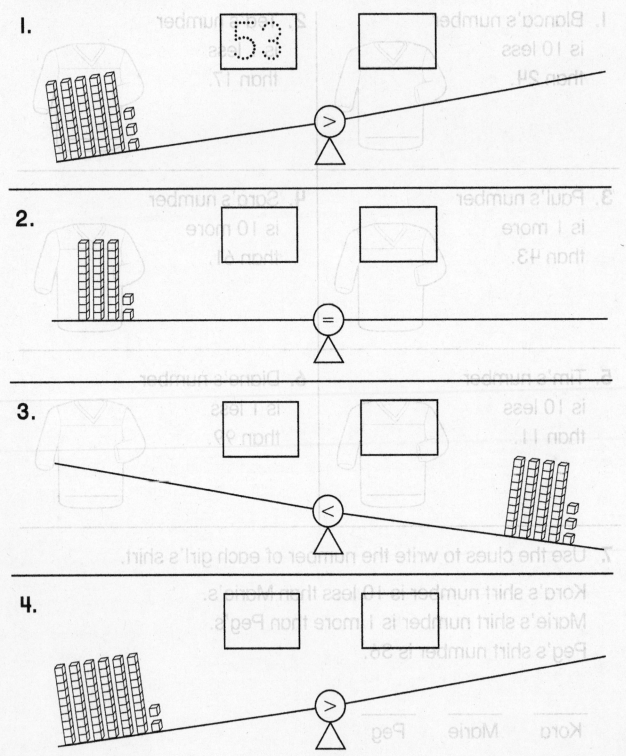

1.

53

2.

3.

4.

Number-Line Estimation: Numbers to 100

Some houses on the number line do not have an address. Look at the number in between those houses. Then write the ten that belongs on the house.

1.

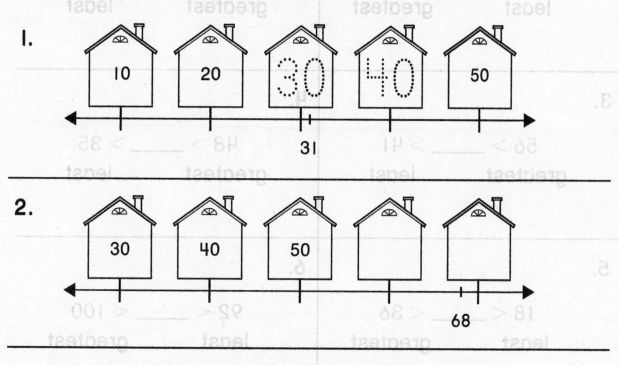

10   20   30   40   50

31

2.

30   40   50

68

3. Draw lines to show where each child goes.

50   60   70   80   90

7 tens 2 ones   5 tens 3 ones   6 tens 5 ones   8 tens 9 ones

Ordering Three Numbers

Write a number that belongs in between.

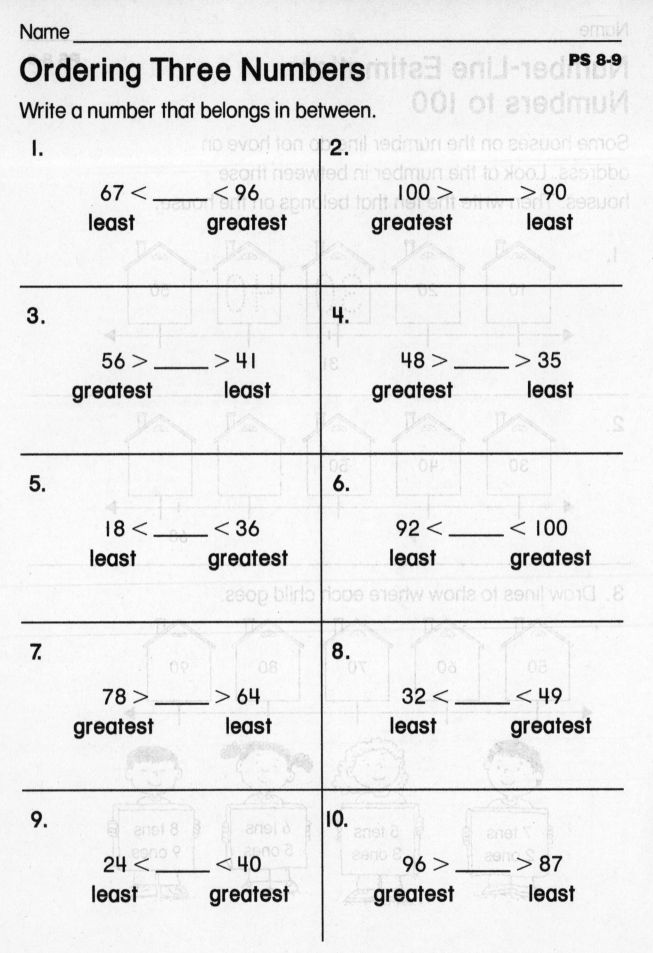

1.

67 < _____ < 96

least   greatest

2.

100 > _____ > 90

greatest   least

3.

56 > _____ > 41

greatest   least

4.

48 > _____ > 35

greatest   least

5.

18 < _____ < 36

least   greatest

6.

92 < _____ < 100

least   greatest

7.

78 > _____ > 64

greatest   least

8.

32 < _____ < 49

least   greatest

9.

24 < _____ < 40

least   greatest

10.

96 > _____ > 87

greatest   least

Hundreds

Write the number that matches the clues.

1. I have 5 hundreds.
I have 6 tens.
I have 1 one.
What number am I?

_____   _____   _____   =   _____
hundreds   tens   ones

2. I have 2 hundreds.
I have 5 tens.
I have 3 ones.
What number am I?

_____   _____   _____   =   _____
hundreds   tens   ones

3. I have 3 hundreds.
I have 9 tens.
I have 8 ones.
What number am I?

_____   _____   _____   =   _____
hundreds   tens   ones

4. I have 6 hundreds.
I have 4 tens.
I have 8 ones.
What number am I?

_____   _____   _____   =   _____
hundreds   tens   ones

5. Write the missing numbers in the chart.

391		393	394		396	397			400
401			404	405	406				410
	412			415				419	420
	422				426		428	429	

Sorting

Lizzie has two fish tanks.
How can Lizzie sort the fish?

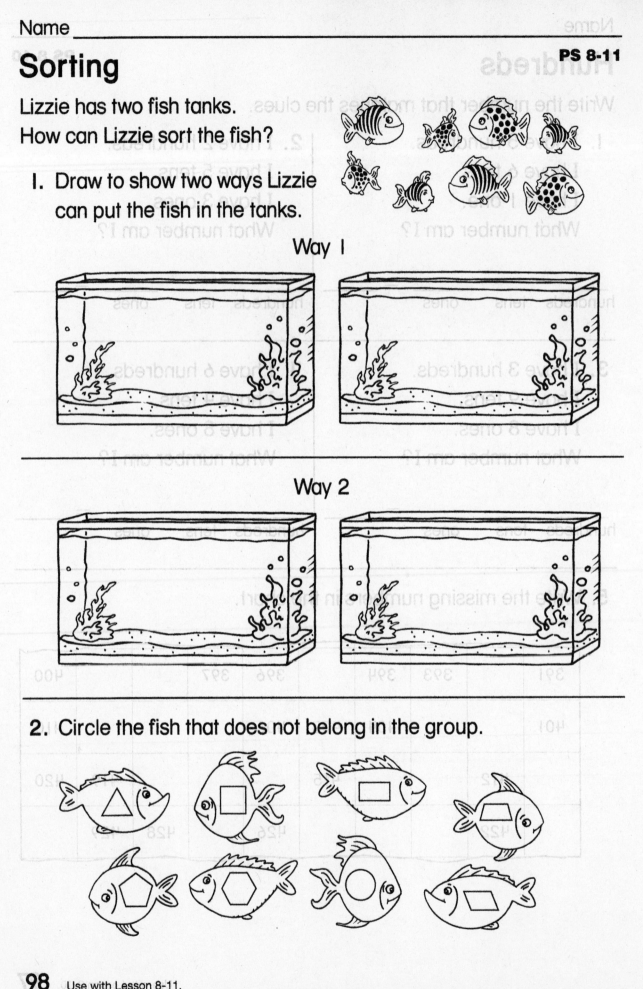

1. Draw to show two ways Lizzie
   can put the fish in the tanks.

Way 1

Way 2

2. Circle the fish that does not belong in the group.

Making Graphs

The graph shows the ways the children get to school.

How We Get to School							
🚌 School Bus	🚌	🚌	🚌	🚌	🚌		
🚗 Car		🚗	🚗	🚗			
👟 Walk		👟	👟	👟	👟	👟	👟

Use the graph to answer the questions.

1. How do most children get to school? _____

2. By which way do the least children get to school? _____

3. Which way did more children get to school, by car or by walking? _____

4. How many fewer children walk to school than ride in a school bus or car? _____

Writing in Math

5. Write a question about the picture graph above.

_____

_____

Making Bar Graphs

Which holiday is the favorite of your class?
Make a bar graph to find out.

Our Favorite Holidays										
♡ Valentine's Day										
🏳 4th of July										
🦃 Thanksgiving										
	1	2	3	4	5	6	7	8	9	10

Ask your classmates to select their favorite holiday.
Color to make a bar graph.
Then use the graph to answer the questions.

1. Which holiday is the favorite of your class?

   _____

2. Which holiday was the least favorite?

   _____

3. Which holiday was selected more,
   Valentine's Day or Thanksgiving? _____

4. How may children would have
   selected Thanksgiving if
   two more children had selected it? _____

5. Put the holidays in order from **least** to **greatest**
   according to the number of spaces colored.

   _____ _____ _____
   least   **greatest**

© Pearson Education, Inc. 1

Name _____

Using Tally Marks

Your class is having a pizza party. What toppings will you get on the pizza? Ask classmates which **two** toppings they want. Make a tally mark for each answer. Write the totals.

Pizza Toppings

		Total
Extra Cheese		
Pepperoni		
Onions		
Mushrooms		

Use the tally chart to answer the questions.

1. Which topping was selected the most?

   _____

2. Which topping was selected the least?

   _____

3. How many children want pepperoni? _____

4. How many children want pepperoni and extra cheese altogether? _____

   _____

Writing in Math

5. Write your own question about the tally chart.

   _____

Coordinate Grids

This is a map of your town.

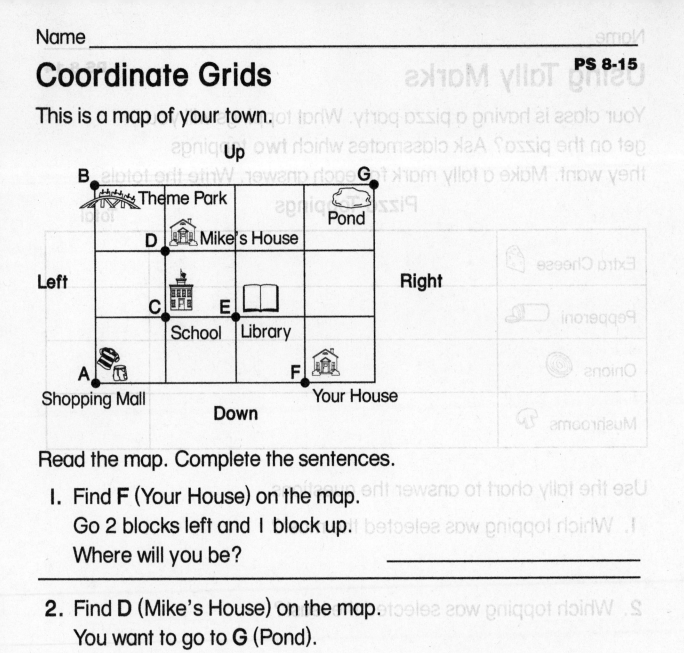

Read the map. Complete the sentences.

1. Find **F** (Your House) on the map.
   Go 2 blocks left and 1 block up.
   Where will you be? _____

2. Find **D** (Mike's House) on the map.
   You want to go to **G** (Pond).

   You will go _____ blocks right and _____ block up.

3. You are at **B** (Theme Park). You want
   to go to **F** (Your House).

   You will go _____ blocks right and _____ blocks down.

4. Find **E** (Library) on the map.
   Go 2 blocks left and 1 block down.
   Where will you be? _____

Name _____

Use Data from a Map

This is a map of Ben's neighborhood.

Find the shortest path from Ben's house to the school. Write an addition sentence.

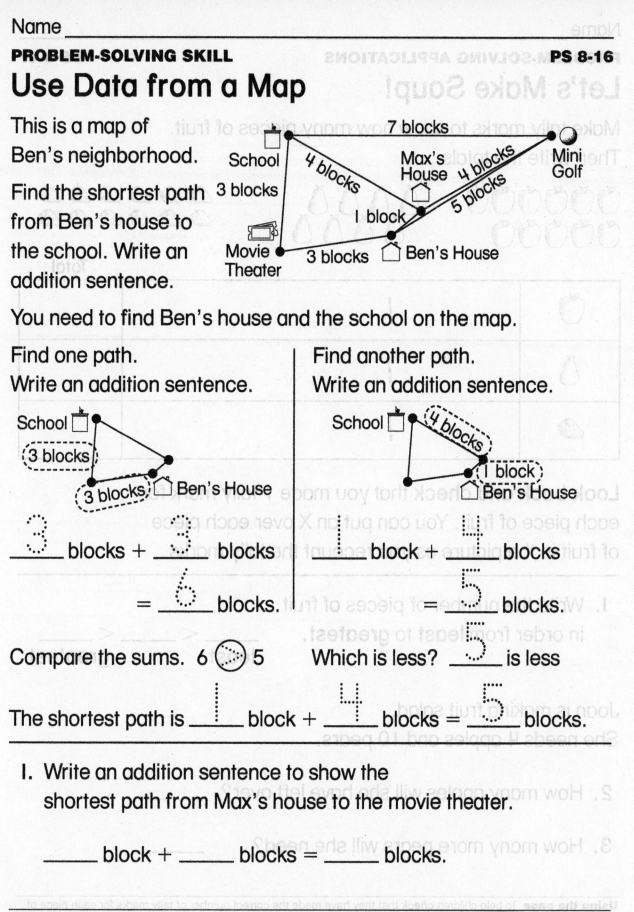

You need to find Ben's house and the school on the map.

Find one path.
Write an addition sentence.

Find another path.
Write an addition sentence.

_3_ blocks + _3_ blocks

= _6_ blocks.

_1_ block + _4_ blocks

= _5_ blocks.

Compare the sums. 6 (>) 5   Which is less? _5_ is less

The shortest path is _1_ block + _4_ blocks = _5_ blocks.

---

1. Write an addition sentence to show the shortest path from Max's house to the movie theater.

_____ block + _____ blocks = _____ blocks.

Using the page *Read* the problem with the children. Then look at the map. Point out that there is more than one way to reach the destination. Be sure children *understand* that they are to find the shortest path.

PROBLEM-SOLVING APPLICATIONS

Let's Make Soup!

Make tally marks to show how many pieces of fruit.
Then write the totals.

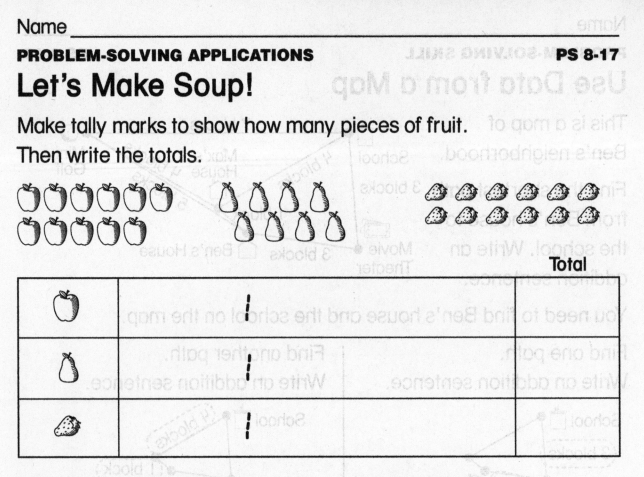

		Total
🍎	I	
🍐	I	
🍓	I	

Look back and check that you made I tally mark for
each piece of fruit. You can put an X over each piece
of fruit in the picture as you recount the tally marks.

_____

1. Write the number of pieces of fruit
   in order from **least** to **greatest**. ____ < ____ < ____

                                                          least   **greatest**

Joan is making fruit salad.
She needs 4 apples and 10 pears.

2. How many apples will she have left over? _____

3. How many more pears will she need? _____

_____

Using the page To help children **check** that they have made the correct number of tally marks for each piece of
fruit, have them **look back** at the pictures of the fruit, count the number of each type, and **check** that their count
matches the number they wrote on the tally chart.

104 Use with Lesson 8-17.

Nickel and Penny

The children have the same amount of money.
Show the money two ways.
Circle one way in red.
Circle the other way in blue.

1. Jim and Kim
   each have

   | 6¢ |

2. Jane and Shane
   each have

   | 9¢ |

3. Nan and Dan
   each have

   | 11¢ |

4. Write the price for each toy.
   Remember, the price of the plane
   must stay the same.

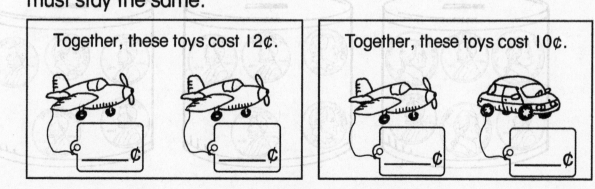

Together, these toys cost 12¢.

_____ ¢   _____ ¢

Together, these toys cost 10¢.

_____ ¢   _____ ¢

Dime

Each child has dimes and pennies.
Read each story. Then mark **D** for dime
and **P** for penny to show how many
dimes and how many pennies.

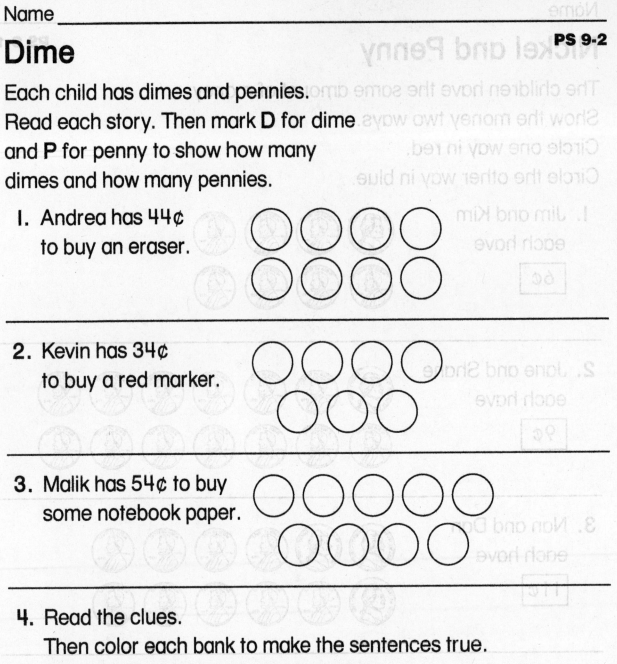

1. Andrea has 44¢
   to buy an eraser.

2. Kevin has 34¢
   to buy a red marker.

3. Malik has 54¢ to buy
   some notebook paper.

4. Read the clues.
   Then color each bank to make the sentences true.
   The orange bank has the most money.
   The purple bank has more money than the yellow bank.

Counting Dimes and Nickels

Draw dimes and nickels to show
the amount in two ways.
Circle the way that uses the fewest coins.

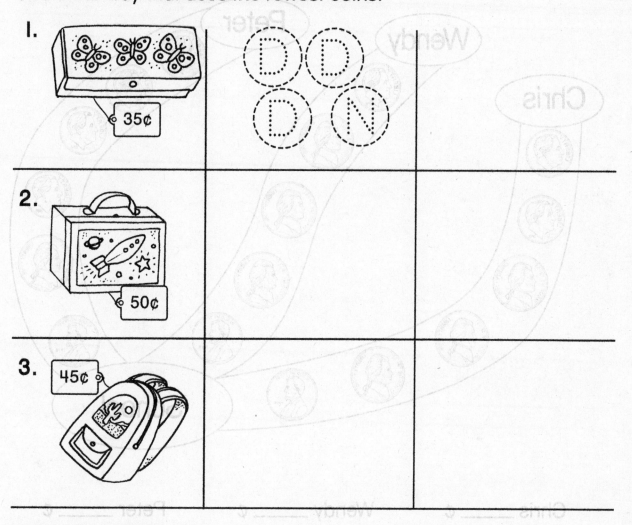

Solve the riddles.

4. Miranda has 6 coins.
   She has 2 dimes.
   The rest are nickels.
   How much money
   does she have?

   _____ ¢

5. Raymond has 6 coins.
   He has 2 nickels.
   The rest are dimes.
   How much money
   does he have?

   _____ ¢

Counting Dimes, Nickels, and Pennies PS 9-4

How much money did each child find on the way to school? Count on. Write how much money in all.

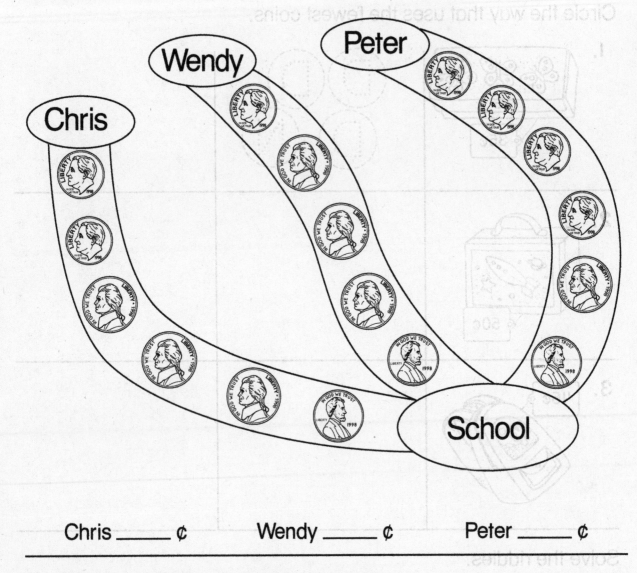

Chris _____ ¢   Wendy _____ ¢   Peter _____ ¢

I. There are 5 coins in Karen's pocket.
Some are dimes and some are pennies.

What is the greatest amount of money
Karen could have?   _____ ¢

What is the least amount of money
Karen could have?   _____ ¢

Name _____

Use Data from a Table

Michael buys a pencil case.

He pays with 1 dime.

Will Michael get change? Write **yes** or **no**.

How much is a pencil case?

Look at the table. __9__ ¢

How much did he pay? __10__ ¢

Price List	
✏ Pencil	8¢
◇ Eraser	4¢
📓 Notebook	11¢
▭ Pencil Case	9¢

He pays more than the price. Will he get change? __yes__

_____

Use the price list above. Write **yes** or **no**.

1. You buy a pencil and an eraser.
   You pay with 2 nickels and 2 pennies.

   Will you get change? _____

   The price is __8__ + __4__ = _____ ¢. You pay _____ ¢.

_____

2. You buy a notebook and a pencil.
   You pay with 2 dimes.

   Will you get change? _____

   The price is _____ + _____ = _____ ¢. You pay _____ ¢.

_____

Writing in Math

3. Write a story problem using the
   information from the price list. _____

_____

Using the page *Read* each story with the children. To help them *understand,* have them find the item being
bought and its price on the table, then compare that price to the amount that is paid to solve the problem.

Name _____

Quarter

Each child has 25¢.

Label the coins to show which coins they have.

1. Ben has 5 coins.

   One is a nickel.

   What are the other coins?

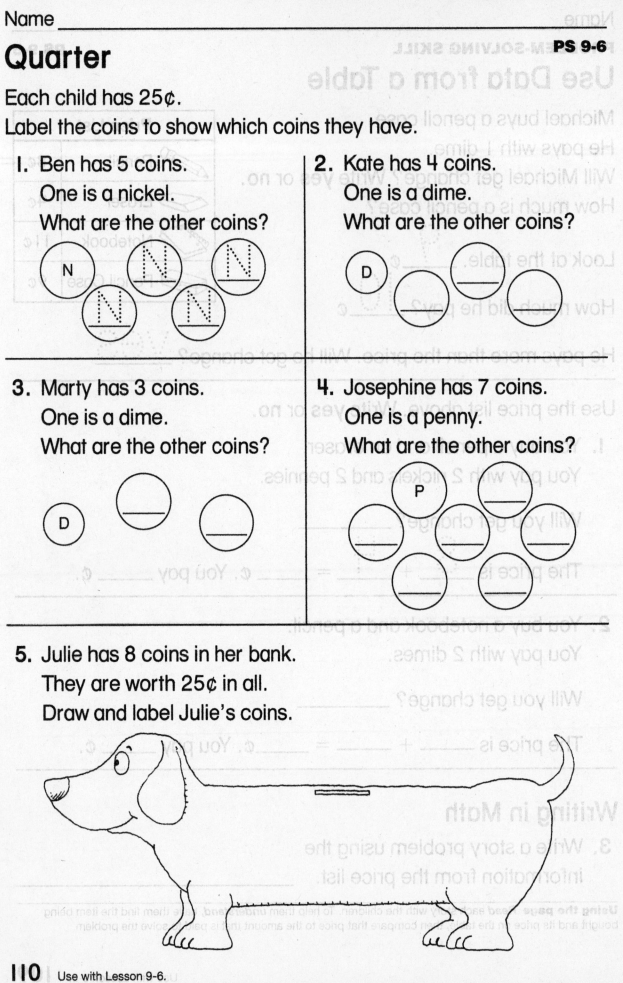

2. Kate has 4 coins.

   One is a dime.

   What are the other coins?

3. Marty has 3 coins.

   One is a dime.

   What are the other coins?

4. Josephine has 7 coins.

   One is a penny.

   What are the other coins?

5. Julie has 8 coins in her bank.

   They are worth 25¢ in all.

   Draw and label Julie's coins.

Counting Sets of Coins

Count the coins in the change purse.

Write the amount.

Then show the same amount using fewer coins.

Draw and label coins in the empty change purse.

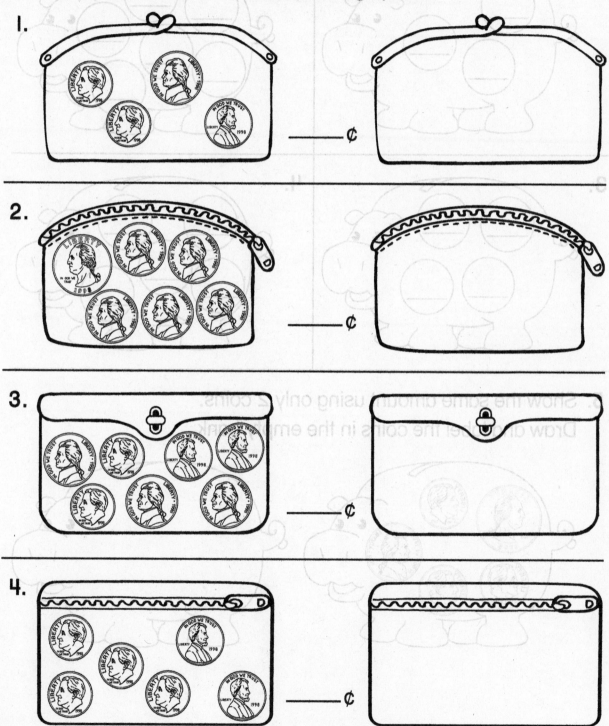

1. _____ ¢

2. _____ ¢

3. _____ ¢

4. _____ ¢

Half-Dollar and Dollar

There is $1.00 in each piggy bank.
Label the coins to show $1.00.

1.

2.

3.

4.

5. Show the same amount using only 2 coins.
   Draw and label the coins in the empty bank.

PROBLEM-SOLVING STRATEGY

Try, Check, and Revise

car 8¢ doll 10¢ bear 6¢ ball 5¢

Jamal buys 2 toys.

The total amount was 14¢.

Which toys did he buy?

__8__ + __5__ = __13__ ¢.

13¢ is less than 14¢. Try again.

__8__ + __6__ = __14__ ¢.

Jamal bought the __car__ and __bear__.

___

Write the toys each child bought.

Then write an addition sentence to check your guess.

1. Cindy bought 2 toys.

   Together they cost 15¢.

   What did she buy?   _____ + _____ = _____ ¢

   _____   _____

2. Sid bought 2 toys.

   Together they cost 11¢.

   What toys did he buy?   _____ + _____ = _____ ¢

   _____   _____

Using the page Have children *look back and check* that the cost of the two toys they chose is the same as the total amount spent by each child. If your total amount is less than (or greater than) the child's amount, try different combinations of toys.

Name _____

What Can You Buy?

Circle the coins you need to
buy the bag of raisins.

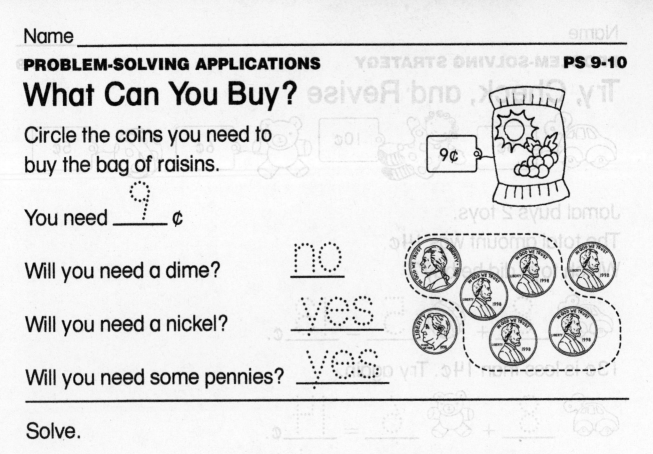

9¢

You need ___9___ ¢

Will you need a dime?   no

Will you need a nickel?   yes

Will you need some pennies?   yes

Solve.

1. Circle the coins you will need to buy 2 bags of raisins.

2. Circle the coins you will need to buy an apple.

24¢

Using the page To help children *plan and solve* have them count the coins and circle the amount of money
they need.

Estimating, Measuring, and Comparing Length

Measure each object using cubes.

Color the longest object red.

Color the shortest object blue.

1.

about _____ cubes

orange

about _____ cubes

about _____ cubes

2. John wants to put the objects into this box.

In which space does each thing go? Write the name.

PROBLEM-SOLVING STRATEGY PS 10-2

Use Logical Reasoning

Predict: Will you need more paper clips or more cubes to measure the paint brush?

more 🖇 more 🧊

Think: It takes fewer long objects than short objects to measure something.

Compare the length of the paper clip with the length of the cube.

The __paper clip__ is longer.

It will probably take more __cubes__.

Measure to check your prediction.

1. Predict: Will it take fewer paper clips or fewer cubes to measure the spoon?

fewer 🖇 fewer 🧊

Measure
about _____ 🖇
about _____ 🧊

Using the page Have children *look back and check* by measuring the object first with paper clips and then with cubes.

Estimating and Measuring with Inches PS 10-3

This [_____] is 1 inch long. Read each story.
Estimate where the cut should be and draw a blue
line. Then measure using a ruler and draw a red line.

1. Dan is making a bookmark.
   He needs a piece of paper 4 inches long.

2. Rita needs a piece of ribbon 6 inches long.

3. Sally needs a string 5 inches long.

4. Ken is stringing beads for a necklace.

   Each bead is 1 inch long.

   How long is the necklace after Ken strings 5 beads?

   _____ inches

   How long is the necklace after he strings 11 beads?

   _____ inches

Estimating and Measuring with Feet

Estimate the length or height.

Then ask a friend to help you measure using a ruler.

1. How tall are you?

    Stand next to a wall.

    Have a friend mark your height

    to measure.

> Estimate: I am about _____ feet tall.

    Measure: I am _____ feet tall.

2. What is the length of a friend's arm?

    Have your friend hold up his or her arm to measure.

    Estimate:

    My friend's arm is about _____ feet.

    Measure:

    My friend's arm is _____ feet.

3. About how tall might each object be?

    Circle the better estimate.

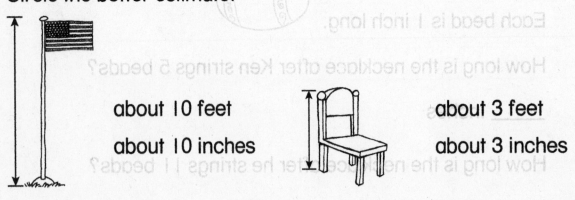

about 10 feet

about 10 inches

about 3 feet

about 3 inches

4. Circle the object that is shorter.

Estimating and Measuring with Centimeters

Draw lines from the star to each dot by the animals.
Then answer the questions. Use a centimeter ruler
to measure.

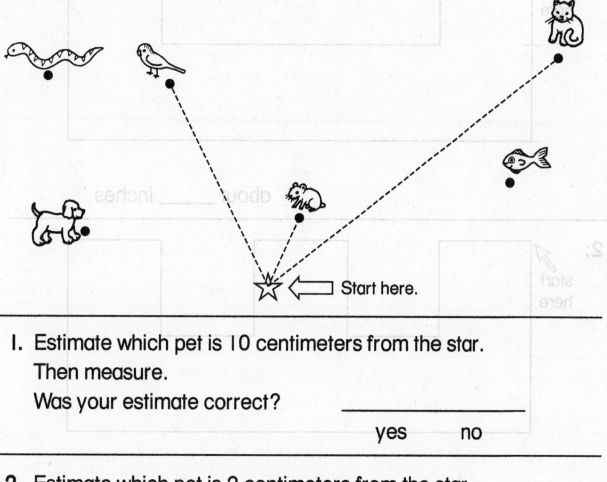

Start here.

1. Estimate which pet is 10 centimeters from the star.
   Then measure.
   Was your estimate correct?   _____

                                      yes   no

2. Estimate which pet is 2 centimeters from the star.
   Then measure.
   Was your estimate correct?   _____

                                      yes   no

3. Estimate which pet is 6 centimeters from the star.
   Then measure.
   Was your estimate correct?   _____

                                      yes   no

Understanding Perimeter

Use a ruler. Mark inches on each side of the shape.
Then count how many inches around each shape.

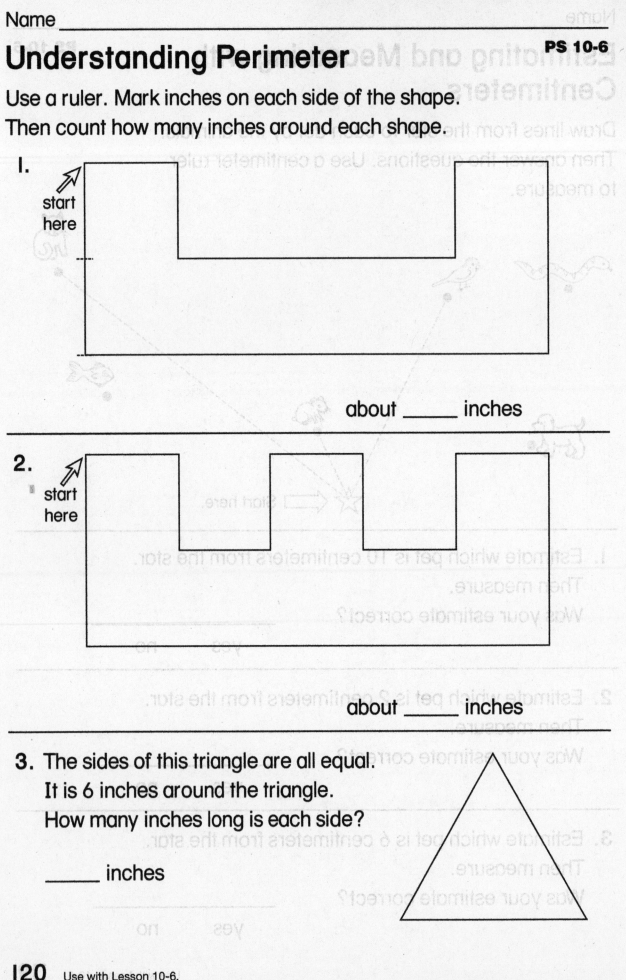

1.

start
here

about _____ inches

2.

start
here

about _____ inches

3. The sides of this triangle are all equal.
It is 6 inches around the triangle.
How many inches long is each side?

_____ inches

Look Back and Check

Tim wants to cover this
shape with cubes.
How many cubes will he need?
Try 4 cubes. Is that enough?

yes   (no)

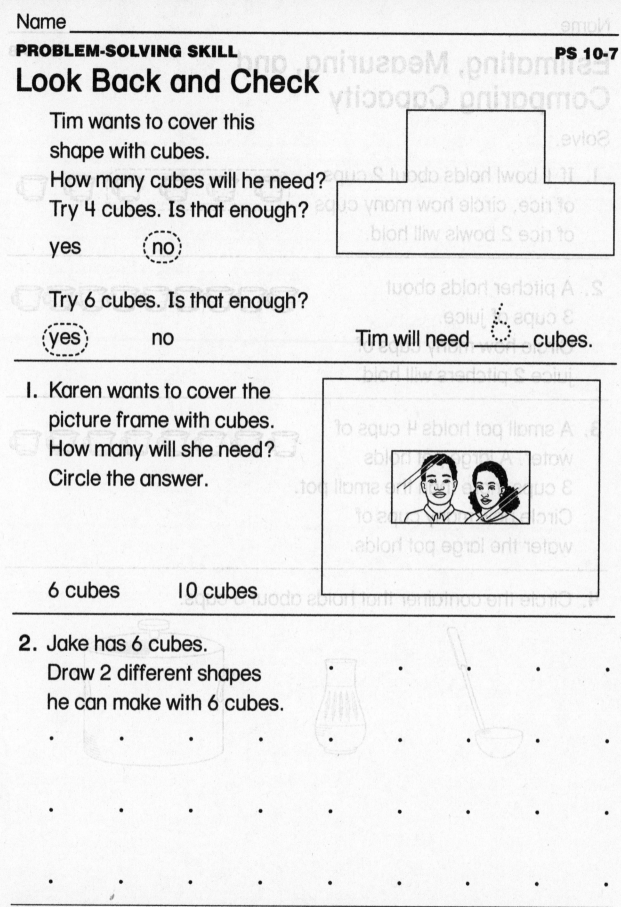

Try 6 cubes. Is that enough?

(yes)   no   Tim will need ___6___ cubes.

---

1. Karen wants to cover the
   picture frame with cubes.
   How many will she need?
   Circle the answer.

   6 cubes   10 cubes

---

2. Jake has 6 cubes.
   Draw 2 different shapes
   he can make with 6 cubes.

Using the page Help children **plan and solve** by pointing out that they can try to cover the shape with some
cubes. If that amount of cubes is too few or too many, they can try again with more or fewer cubes.

Estimating, Measuring, and Comparing Capacity

Solve.

1. If 1 bowl holds about 2 cups of rice, circle how many cups of rice 2 bowls will hold.

2. A pitcher holds about 3 cups of juice. Circle how many cups of juice 2 pitchers will hold.

3. A small pot holds 4 cups of water. A large pot holds 3 cups more than the small pot. Circle how many cups of water the large pot holds.

4. Circle the container that holds about 3 cups.

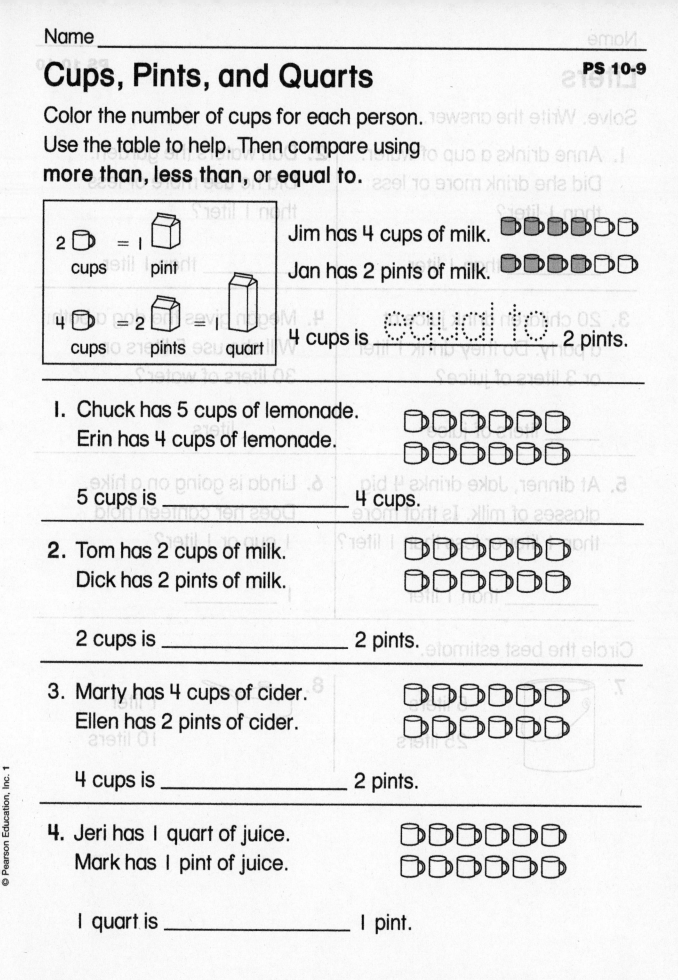

Name _____

Cups, Pints, and Quarts

Color the number of cups for each person.
Use the table to help. Then compare using
more than, less than, or **equal to.**

Jim has 4 cups of milk.

Jan has 2 pints of milk.

4 cups is ___equal to___ 2 pints.

1. Chuck has 5 cups of lemonade.
   Erin has 4 cups of lemonade.

   5 cups is _____ 4 cups.

2. Tom has 2 cups of milk.
   Dick has 2 pints of milk.

   2 cups is _____ 2 pints.

3. Marty has 4 cups of cider.
   Ellen has 2 pints of cider.

   4 cups is _____ 2 pints.

4. Jeri has 1 quart of juice.
   Mark has 1 pint of juice.

   1 quart is _____ 1 pint.

© Pearson Education, Inc. 1

Liters

Solve. Write the answer.

1. Anne drinks a cup of water. Did she drink more or less than 1 liter?

_____ than 1 liter

2. Dan waters the garden. Did he use more or less than 1 liter?

_____ than 1 liter

3. 20 children drink juice at a party. Do they drink 1 liter or 3 liters of juice?

_____ liters of juice

4. Megan gives the dog a bath. Will she use 5 liters or 30 liters of water?

_____ liters

5. At dinner, Jake drinks 4 big glasses of milk. Is that more than 1 liter or less than 1 liter?

_____ than 1 liter

6. Linda is going on a hike. Does her canteen hold 1 cup or 1 liter?

1 _____

Circle the best estimate.

7.

5 liters

25 liters

8.

1 liter

10 liters

Estimating, Measuring, and Comparing Weight

Does the first object weigh **more than, less than,** or **about the same as** the second object?
Circle your answer.

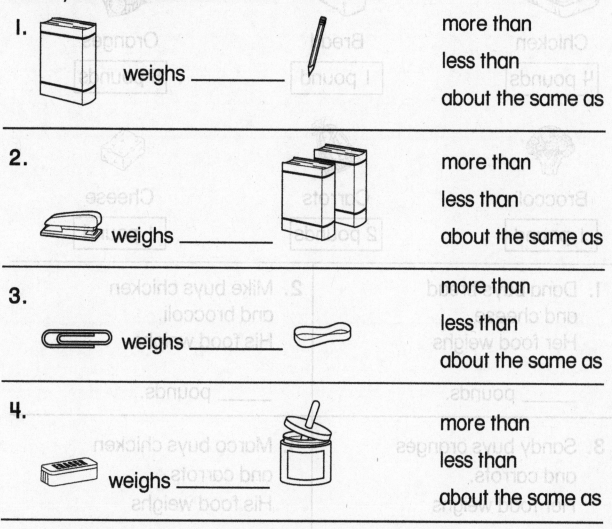

1. _____ weighs _____

more than

less than

about the same as

2. _____ weighs _____

more than

less than

about the same as

3. _____ weighs _____

more than

less than

about the same as

4. _____ weighs _____

more than

less than

about the same as

5. Number the objects from the lightest to heaviest.
   Use I for the lightest and 4 for the heaviest.

_____   _____   _____   _____

Pounds

Look at the weight of each food.
Use the pictures to find out how many pounds in all.

Chicken
| 4 pounds |

Bread
| 1 pound |

Oranges
| 5 pounds |

Broccoli
| 1 pound |

Carrots
| 2 pounds |

Cheese
| 1 pound |

1. Dana buys bread
and cheese.
Her food weighs

_____ pounds.

2. Mike buys chicken
and broccoli.
His food weighs

_____ pounds.

3. Sandy buys oranges
and carrots.
Her food weighs

_____ pounds.

4. Marco buys chicken
and carrots.
His food weighs

_____ pounds.

5. Kevin buys carrots
and broccoli.
His food weighs

_____ pounds.

6. Carrots cost 10¢ for 1 pound.
How much does the bag of
carrots shown above cost?

_____ ¢

Grams and Kilograms

Circle the best estimate.

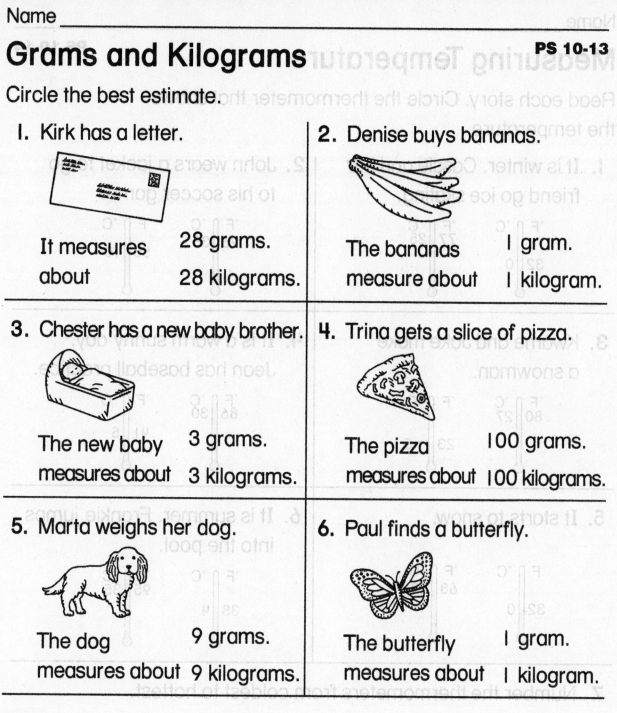

1. Kirk has a letter.

   It measures about

   28 grams.

   28 kilograms.

2. Denise buys bananas.

   The bananas measure about

   1 gram.

   1 kilogram.

3. Chester has a new baby brother.

   The new baby measures about

   3 grams.

   3 kilograms.

4. Trina gets a slice of pizza.

   The pizza measures about

   100 grams.

   100 kilograms.

5. Marta weighs her dog.

   The dog measures about

   9 grams.

   9 kilograms.

6. Paul finds a butterfly.

   The butterfly measures about

   1 gram.

   1 kilogram.

Solve.

7. Sandra has two pencils.

   Together they measure 18 grams.

   One pencil measures 10 grams.

   How much does the other pencil measure?

   10 + _____ = 18 grams

Name _____

Measuring Temperature

Read each story. Circle the thermometer that shows
the temperature.

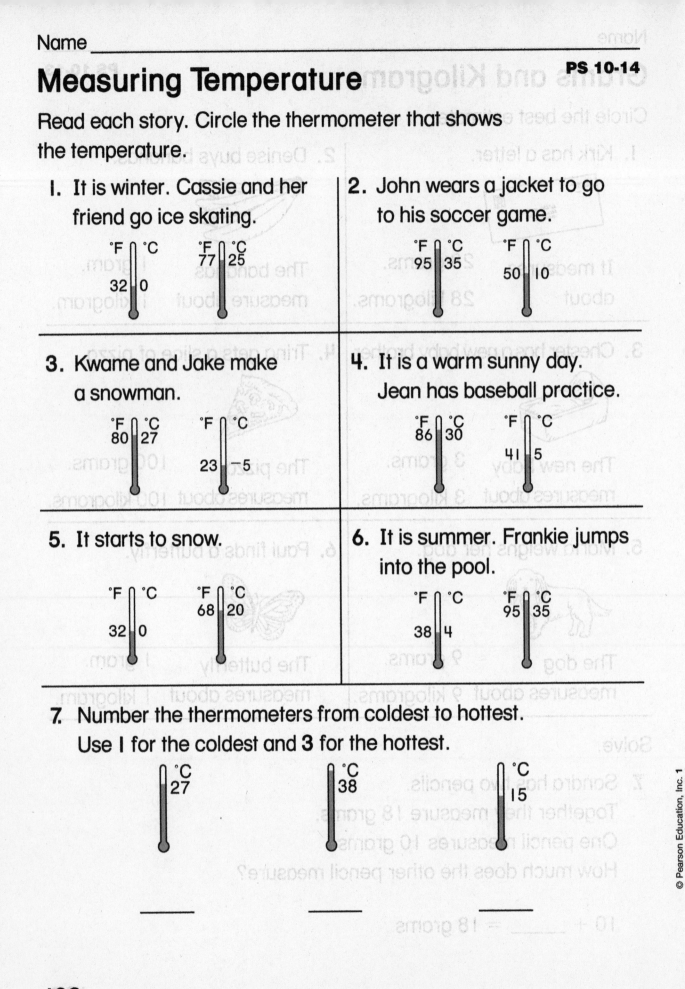

1. It is winter. Cassie and her
friend go ice skating.

°F °C   °F °C
        77 25
32 0

2. John wears a jacket to go
to his soccer game.

°F °C   °F °C
95 35   50 10

3. Kwame and Jake make
a snowman.

°F °C   °F °C
80 27
        23 -5

4. It is a warm sunny day.
Jean has baseball practice.

°F °C   °F °C
86 30   41 5

5. It starts to snow.

°F °C   °F °C
        68 20
32 0

6. It is summer. Frankie jumps
into the pool.

°F °C   °F °C
        95 35
38 4

7. Number the thermometers from coldest to hottest.
Use **1** for the coldest and **3** for the hottest.

°C   °C   °C
27   38   15

_____   _____   _____

Choosing a Measurement Tool

Eduardo has a new puppy. Circle the best tool to use for the measurement.

1. How much does the puppy weigh?

2. How much food should Eduardo give the puppy to eat?

3. What is the temperature of the room?

4. How long is the puppy?

Draw something you could measure with each tool.

5.

6.

Certain or Impossible

Read each story. Circle **certain** or **impossible**.

1. Julie's garden has only red flowers. Is she certain to pick a yellow flower or is it impossible?

   certain   impossible

2. Eric has 20 model cars on his toy shelf. They are the only toys on the shelf. Eric picks a toy from the shelf. Is he certain to pick a model car or is it impossible?

   certain   impossible

3. Gina has a bag of raisins. Is she certain to pick a raisin from the bag or is it impossible?

   certain   impossible

4. There are only pennies in Trevor's piggy bank. Is he certain to find a dime in the piggy bank or is it impossible?

   certain   impossible

5. Draw 5 coins in the bank. Draw the coins so that it is impossible to pick a penny **and** it is certain that you will pick a dime.

More Likely or Less Likely

Read the story. Circle **more likely** or **less likely**.

1. The school bus has 30 red seats and 10 blue seats. Is it more likely or less likely that Tammy will sit in a red seat?

   more likely   less likely

2. There are 40 purple cubes and 2 green cubes in a bag. Is it more likely or less likely that John will pick a green cube?

   more likely   less likely

3. There are 15 blue cars and 2 white cars in the parking lot. Are you more likely or less likely to see a blue car in the parking lot?

   more likely   less likely

4. Mira has a bag of beads. There are 50 yellow beads and 20 orange beads. Is Mira more likely or less likely to pick a yellow bead from the bag?

   more likely   less likely

Solve.

5. Kathy spun the spinner 15 times. She landed on yellow 10 times. How many times did she land on green?

_____ times

Name _____

Stir Fry It!

Judy is making chicken and rice.
She needs to boil 1 quart of water.
Is 1 quart more than 2 cups
or less than 2 cups?

> Think: 2 cups is
> 1 pint. 1 quart is
> more than 1 pint.

1 quart is ___more___ than 2 cups.

1. Judy uses a large spoon to mix the chicken and rice.
   Her spoon measures about 13 inches long.
   Is 13 inches more than 3 centimeters or
   less than 3 centimeters?

   _____

2. Is 13 inches more than 1 foot or less than 1 foot?

   _____

3. Circle the temperature that the
   chicken and rice will probably be
   when Judy eats it.

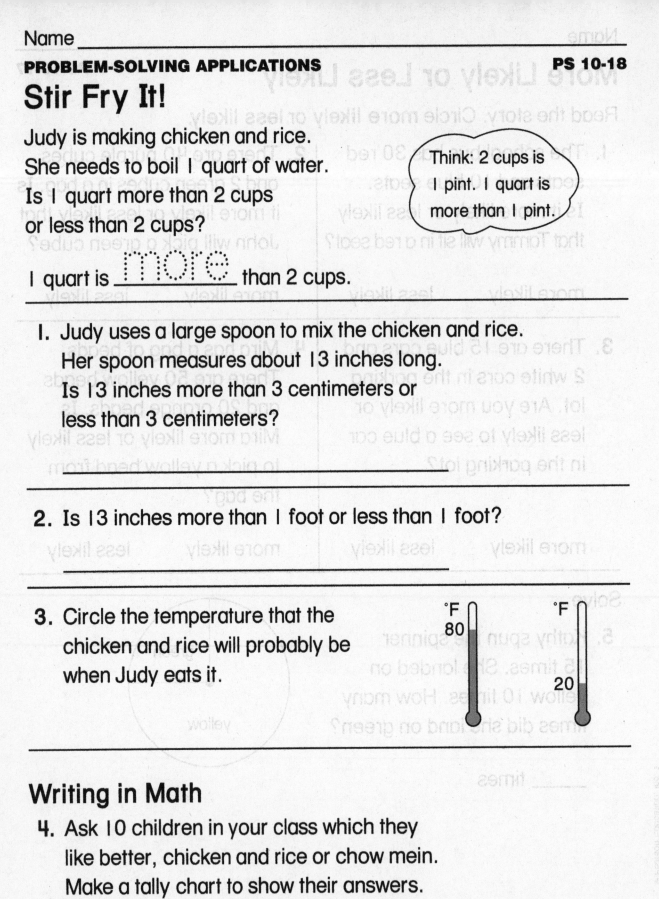

Writing in Math

4. Ask 10 children in your class which they
   like better, chicken and rice or chow mein.
   Make a tally chart to show their answers.

Using the page Help children *read and understand* the exercises by having them restate each exercise in their own words and tell what the exercise is asking them to find.

Doubles

Read each story. Write an addition sentence to solve.

1. The family goes camping. They drive 6 miles to the woods. They drive another 6 miles to the lake. How many miles did they drive in all?

   _____ + _____ = _____

   _____ miles

2. There are 5 cabins near the lake. There are 5 cabins in the woods. How many cabins are there in all?

   _____ + _____ = _____

   _____ cabins

3. The family hikes 9 miles along a path. Then they hike 9 miles back. How many miles did they hike in all?

   _____ + _____ = _____

   _____ miles

4. Mom and Dad make dinner. Mom opens 2 packages of rolls. Each package has 8 rolls. How many rolls are there in all?

   _____ + _____ = _____

   _____ rolls

For each picture write an addition sentence.

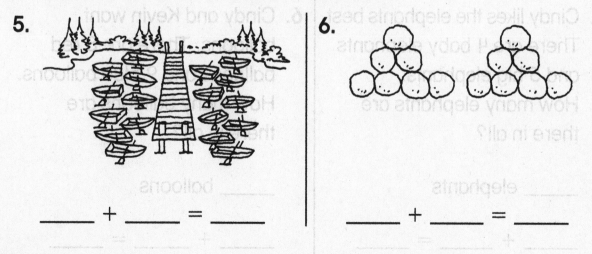

5. _____ + _____ = _____

6. _____ + _____ = _____

Doubles Plus 1 and Doubles Minus 1

Answer each question. Write the doubles fact
you used to help you add.

1. At the circus, 6 dogs ride
a bicycle and 5 dogs ride in
a wagon. How many dogs are
there in all?

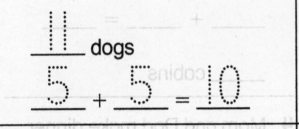

__11__ dogs

__5__ + __5__ = __10__

2. The clown juggles 6 balls.
Then the clown adds 7 more
balls to juggle. How many
balls does the clown juggle
altogether?

_____ balls

____ + ____ = ____

3. 8 clowns get out of a little car.
Then 7 more clowns get out.
How many clowns get out of
the car altogether?

_____ clowns

____ + ____ = ____

4. The animal trainer has
7 lions and 6 tigers.
How many animals does
he have in all?

_____ animals

____ + ____ = ____

5. Cindy likes the elephants best.
There are 4 baby elephants
and 5 big elephants.
How many elephants are
there in all?

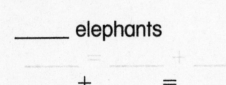

_____ elephants

____ + ____ = ____

6. Cindy and Kevin want
balloons. There are 8 red
balloons and 9 blue balloons.
How many balloons are
there in all?

_____ balloons

____ + ____ = ____

Adding 10

Draw the counters. Then write
a number sentence to solve.

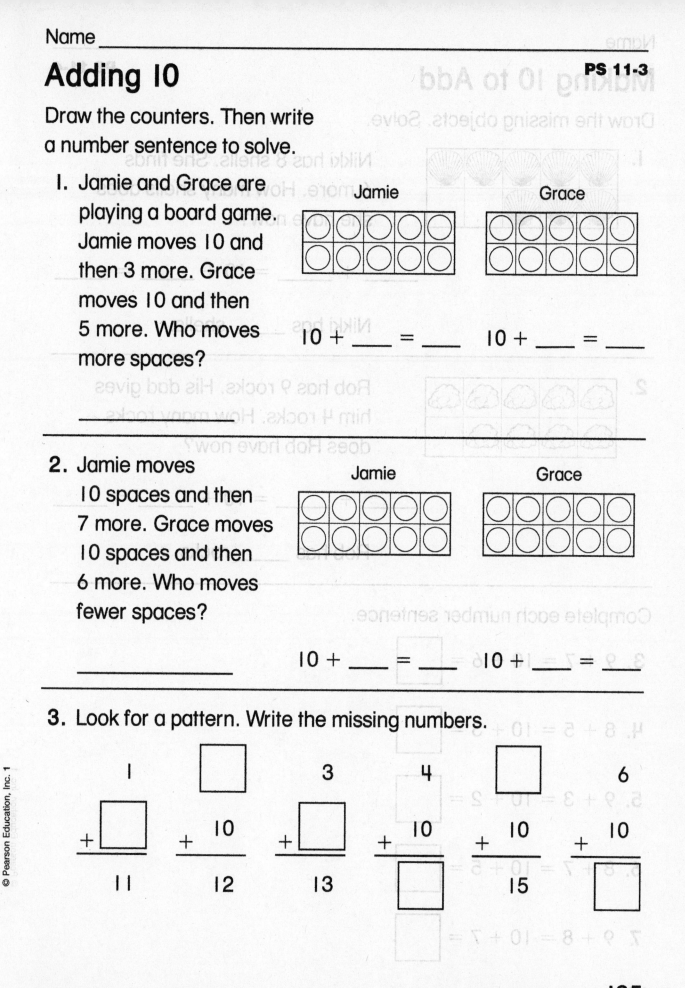

1. Jamie and Grace are
playing a board game.
Jamie moves 10 and
then 3 more. Grace
moves 10 and then
5 more. Who moves
more spaces?

Jamie   Grace

10 + ___ = ___   10 + ___ = ___

_____

2. Jamie moves
10 spaces and then
7 more. Grace moves
10 spaces and then
6 more. Who moves
fewer spaces?

Jamie   Grace

_____

10 + ___ = ___   10 + ___ = ___

3. Look for a pattern. Write the missing numbers.

```
    1         ☐         3         4         ☐         6
  + ☐       + 10      + ☐       + 10      + 10      + 10
  ─────     ─────     ─────     ─────     ─────     ─────
   11        12        13        ☐         15        ☐
```

Making 10 to Add

Draw the missing objects. Solve.

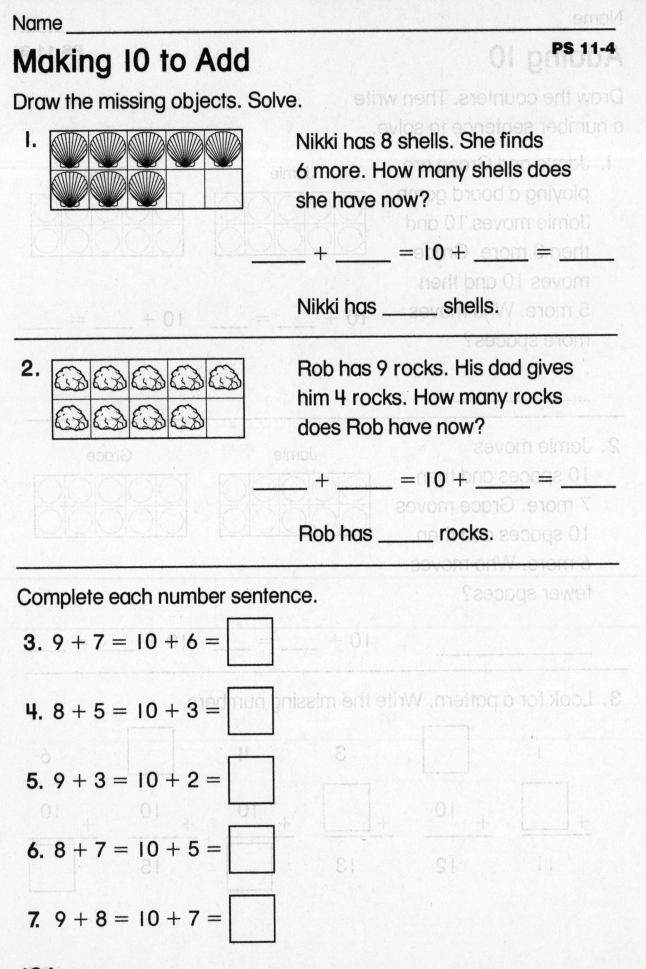

1. Nikki has 8 shells. She finds 6 more. How many shells does she have now?

____ + ____ = 10 + ____ = ____

Nikki has ____ shells.

2. Rob has 9 rocks. His dad gives him 4 rocks. How many rocks does Rob have now?

____ + ____ = 10 + ____ = ____

Rob has ____ rocks.

Complete each number sentence.

3. 9 + 7 = 10 + 6 = ▢

4. 8 + 5 = 10 + 3 = ▢

5. 9 + 3 = 10 + 2 = ▢

6. 8 + 7 = 10 + 5 = ▢

7. 9 + 8 = 10 + 7 = ▢

Applying Addition Fact Strategies

Add. Circle the strategy you used.

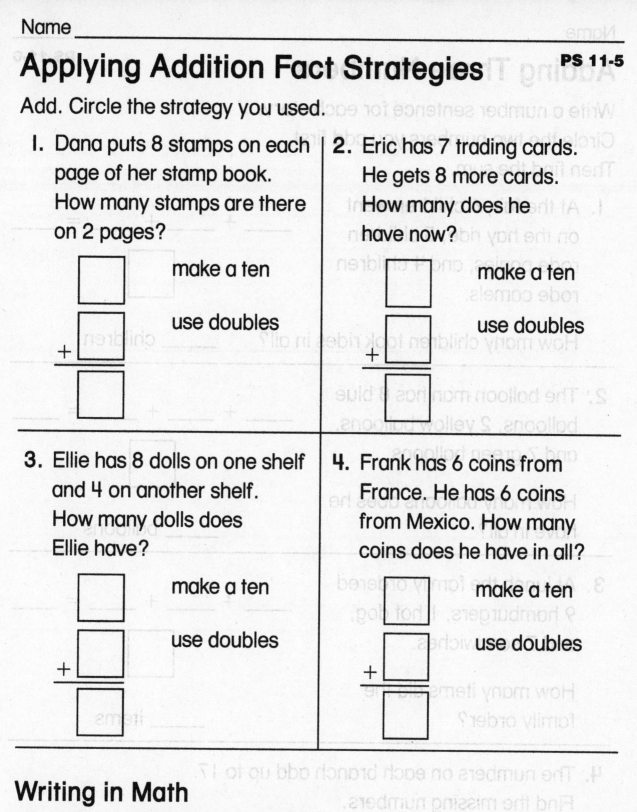

1. Dana puts 8 stamps on each page of her stamp book. How many stamps are there on 2 pages?

    make a ten

    use doubles

2. Eric has 7 trading cards. He gets 8 more cards. How many does he have now?

    make a ten

    use doubles

3. Ellie has 8 dolls on one shelf and 4 on another shelf. How many dolls does Ellie have?

    make a ten

    use doubles

4. Frank has 6 coins from France. He has 6 coins from Mexico. How many coins does he have in all?

    make a ten

    use doubles

Writing in Math

5. Write a story problem that can be solved by using doubles or making a ten.

    _____

    _____

    _____

Name _____

Adding Three Numbers

Write a number sentence for each story.
Circle the two numbers you add first.
Then find the sum.

1. At the fair, 6 children went
   on the hay ride, 5 children
   rode ponies, and 4 children
   rode camels.

   ___ + ___ + ___ = ___

   ☐

   How many children took rides in all? ___ children

2. The balloon man has 8 blue
   balloons, 2 yellow balloons,
   and 7 green balloons.

   ___ + ___ + ___ = ___

   ☐

   How many balloons does he
   have in all? ___ balloons

3. At lunch the family ordered
   9 hamburgers, 1 hot dog,
   and 7 sandwiches.

   ___ + ___ + ___ = ___

   ☐

   How many items did the
   family order? ___ items

4. The numbers on each branch add up to 17.
   Find the missing numbers.

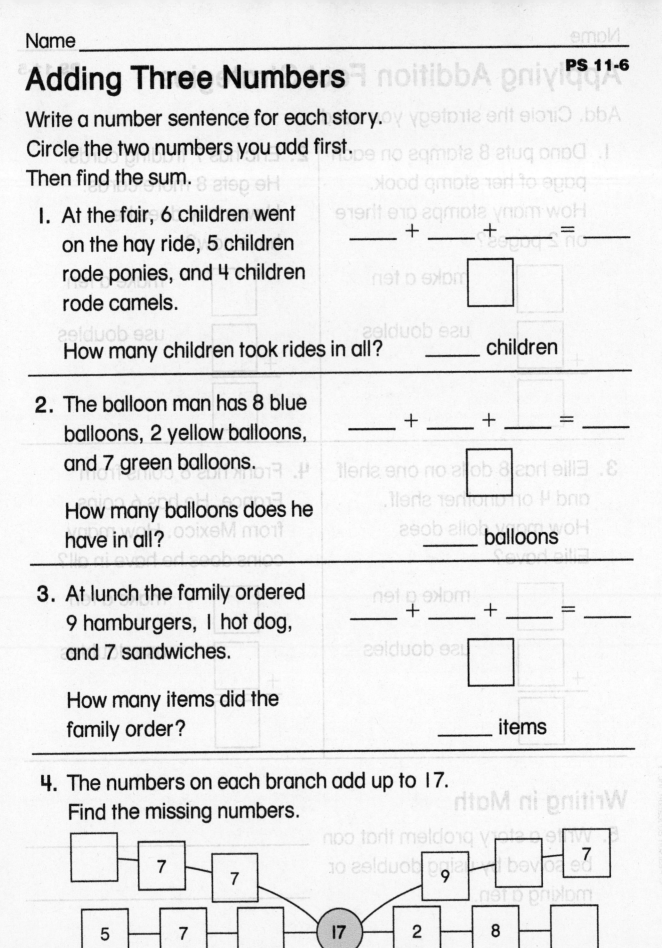

PROBLEM-SOLVING STRATEGY PS 11-7
Make a Table

Dan has a red sock, a yellow sock, a blue sock, and a white sock. He likes to wear different colors together. How many different ways can Dan wear the 4 socks?

You can make a table.

Write: **R** for red

B for blue

W for white

Y for yellow

#1	#2
R	B
R	W
R	Y
B	W

Find all the different ways.

Complete the table.

Dan can wear the socks _____ different ways.

Check to make sure you found all the ways.

---

1. How many different ways can Dan wear socks with just a green sock, a purple sock, and a yellow sock?

_____ different ways

#1	#2

Using the page Help children **plan and solve** by identifying the different ways the colors can be put together and writing them on the chart.

Using Related Facts

Add to solve the first part of the story. Then write a
related subtraction fact to solve the rest of the story.

1. There are 6 children reading at one table and
   7 children reading at another table.
   How many children are reading in all?

   $6 + 7 =$ _____   _____ children

   If 6 children leave, how many will be left?

   _____ – _____ = _____   _____ children

2. Kyle reads 9 books about baseball.
   Mark reads 5 books about dinosaurs.
   How many books did the boys read?

   $9 + 5 =$ _____   _____ books

   How many books were **not** about baseball?

   _____ – _____ = _____   _____ books

3. Tammy read 8 books last month.
   She read 4 this month.
   How many books did Tammy read?

   $8 + 4 =$ _____   _____ books

   If 4 of the books were dog stories,
   how many were **not** dog stories?

   _____ – _____ = _____   _____ books

Fact Families

PS 11-9

Write a fact family about each picture.
Then circle one of the facts and write a story about it.

1.

_____ + _____ = _____

_____ + _____ = _____

_____ − _____ = _____

_____ − _____ = _____

_____

_____

_____

2.

_____ + _____ = _____

_____ + _____ = _____

_____ − _____ = _____

_____ − _____ = _____

_____

_____

_____

Using Addition to Subtract

Circle the addition fact that will help you subtract.
Then write a subtraction sentence to solve.

1. Mike had 14 peanuts. He fed 9 peanuts to the monkeys. How many peanuts does Mike have left?

$9 + 5 = 14$

$9 + 6 = 15$

_____ peanuts

_____ – _____ = _____

2. There are 15 children at the zoo. If 8 children want to see lions and the others want to see zebras, how many children want to see zebras?

$8 + 6 = 14$

$8 + 7 = 15$

_____ children

_____ – _____ = _____

3. Rick has 16¢. He buys a zoo pin for 9¢. How much does he have left?

$9 + 8 = 17$

$9 + 7 = 16$

_____¢

_____¢ – _____¢ = _____¢

4. Mark gave 9 animal stickers to Jody. Mark had 15 animal stickers in all. How many animal stickers does Mark have left?

_____ animal stickers

Using 10 to Subtract

Cross out to subtract. Use a ten frame
and counters if you like.

1. Carmen has 12 grapes.
   She eats 7.
   How many grapes are left?

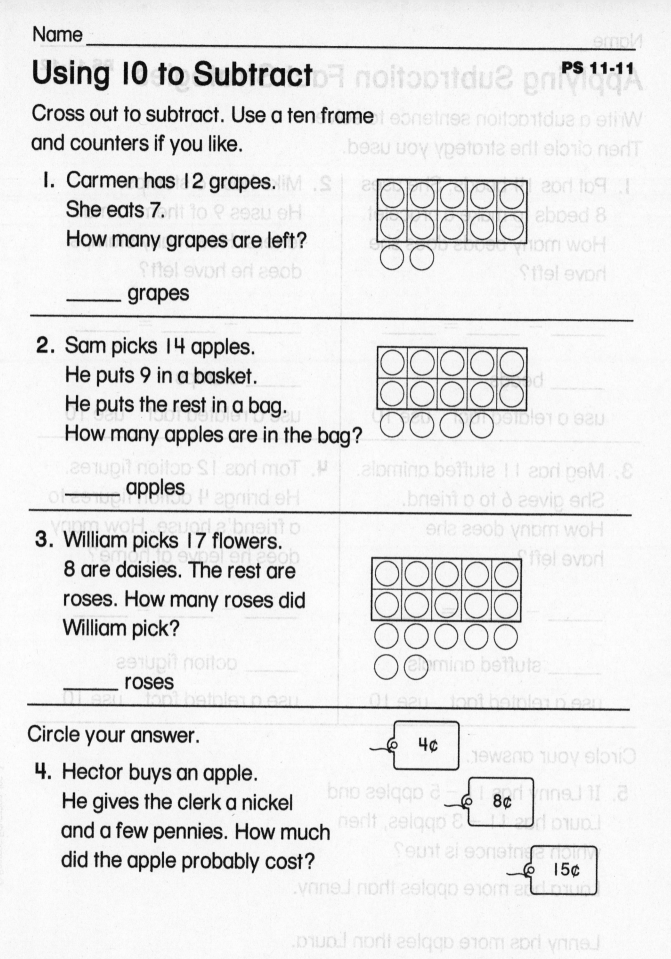

   _____ grapes

2. Sam picks 14 apples.
   He puts 9 in a basket.
   He puts the rest in a bag.
   How many apples are in the bag?

   _____ apples

3. William picks 17 flowers.
   8 are daisies. The rest are
   roses. How many roses did
   William pick?

   _____ roses

Circle your answer.

4. Hector buys an apple.
   He gives the clerk a nickel
   and a few pennies. How much
   did the apple probably cost?

   4¢

   8¢

   15¢

Applying Subtraction Fact Strategies

Write a subtraction sentence to solve.
Then circle the strategy you used.

1. Pat has 14 beads. She uses 8 beads to make a bracelet. How many beads does she have left?

_____ – _____ = _____

_____ beads

use a related fact   use 10

2. Mike has 16 stamps. He uses 9 of them to mail letters. How many stamps does he have left?

_____ – _____ = _____

_____ stamps

use a related fact   use 10

3. Meg has 11 stuffed animals. She gives 6 to a friend. How many does she have left?

_____ – _____ = _____

_____ stuffed animals

use a related fact   use 10

4. Tom has 12 action figures. He brings 4 action figures to a friend's house. How many does he leave at home?

_____ – _____ = _____

_____ action figures

use a related fact   use 10

Circle your answer.

5. If Lenny has 11 − 5 apples and Laura has 11 − 3 apples, then which sentence is true?

Laura has more apples than Lenny.

Lenny has more apples than Laura.

Name _____

Multiple-Step Problems

There are 8 white puppies in the pet store.

There are 7 brown puppies.

How many puppies are in the pet store in all?

Solve the first part of the problem. Then use the answer to solve the second part of the problem.

$$\underline{8} \; \oplus \; \underline{7} \; = \; \underline{15}$$

There are 6 puppies sold.

How many puppies are left?

| How many puppies did the pet shop have? | How many puppies were sold? | How many puppies are left? |

$$\underline{15} \; \ominus \; \underline{6} \; = \; \underline{9} \text{ puppies}$$

Solve.

1. Billy buys 6 cans of dog food. He buys 9 cans of cat food. How many cans of pet food does Billy buy in all?

_____ ◯ _____ = _____ cans

Billy has used 8 cans of pet food. How many cans of pet food does he have left?

_____ ◯ _____ = _____ cans

2. The pet shop has 6 green parakeets. It has 3 yellow parakeets. How many parakeets does the pet shop have in all?

_____ ◯ _____ = _____ parakeets

The pet store gets 7 more yellow parakeets. Now how many parakeets does the pet store have in all?

_____ ◯ _____ = _____ parakeets

Using the page Help children **read** the problem. Have them stop reading after each part and explain what they must do. This will help children **understand** that they must use the solution from the first part of the problem to solve the second part of the problem.

PROBLEM-SOLVING APPLICATIONS

On the Farm

1. There are 12 hens in the chicken coop.
   4 of the hens are brown.
   How many hens are **not** brown?

   $\underline{12} \bigominus \underline{4} = \underline{8}$

   Which related fact can you use to check your answer?
   Circle your answer.

   $7 + 5 = 12$ $\qquad$ $12 - 3 = 9$ $\qquad$ $\boxed{8 + 4 = 12}$

There are 14 horses on the farm.

2. 8 of the horses are in the pasture. How many horses are **not** in the pasture?

   ___ ◯ ___ = ___

3. 4 horses go to the pasture. How many horses are in the pasture now?

   ___ ◯ ___ = ___

Writing in Math

4. Draw a picture of 16 rabbits.
   Write a subtraction story about your picture.
   Then write a number sentence to go with your picture.

   _____

   ___ ◯ ___ = ___

Using the page Have children *look back and check* their answers by using related facts.

Adding Groups of 10

Look at the sum. Find 3 ways to add tens to make the sum.

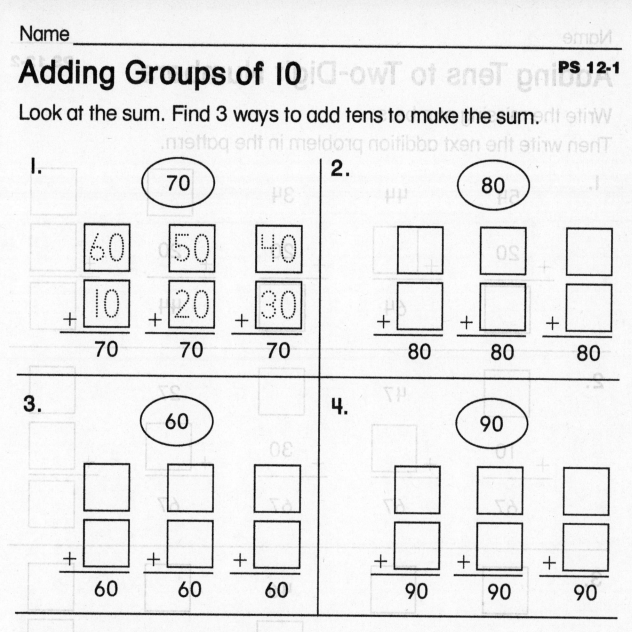

1. (70)

$\begin{array}{r} 60 \\ + 10 \\ \hline 70 \end{array}$ $\begin{array}{r} 50 \\ + 20 \\ \hline 70 \end{array}$ $\begin{array}{r} 40 \\ + 30 \\ \hline 70 \end{array}$

2. (80)

$\begin{array}{r} \square \\ + \square \\ \hline 80 \end{array}$ $\begin{array}{r} \square \\ + \square \\ \hline 80 \end{array}$ $\begin{array}{r} \square \\ + \square \\ \hline 80 \end{array}$

3. (60)

$\begin{array}{r} \square \\ + \square \\ \hline 60 \end{array}$ $\begin{array}{r} \square \\ + \square \\ \hline 60 \end{array}$ $\begin{array}{r} \square \\ + \square \\ \hline 60 \end{array}$

4. (90)

$\begin{array}{r} \square \\ + \square \\ \hline 90 \end{array}$ $\begin{array}{r} \square \\ + \square \\ \hline 90 \end{array}$ $\begin{array}{r} \square \\ + \square \\ \hline 90 \end{array}$

Circle the two groups that answer the question.

5. Randy has 2 groups of coins.

He has more than 80 coins in all.

Which are Randy's coins?

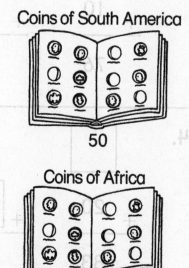

Coins of South America

50

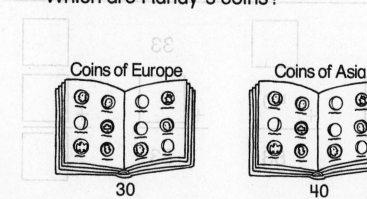

Coins of Europe

30

Coins of Asia

40

Coins of Africa

20

Adding Tens to Two-Digit Numbers

Write the missing numbers.
Then write the next addition problem in the pattern.

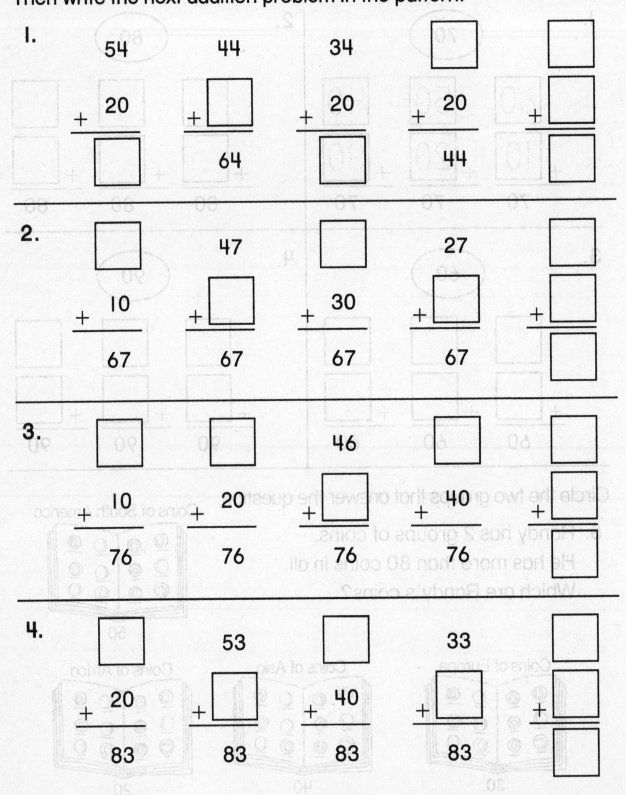

1.

54	44	34	☐(70)	☐
+ 20	+ ☐	+ 20	+ 20	+ ☐
☐	64	☐	44	☐

2.

☐	47	☐	27	☐
+ 10	+ ☐	+ 30	+ ☐	+ ☐
67	67	67	67	☐

3.

☐	☐	46	☐	☐
+ 10	+ 20	+ ☐	+ 40	+ ☐
76	76	76	76	☐

4.

☐	53	☐	33	☐
+ 20	+ ☐	+ 40	+ ☐	+ ☐
83	83	83	83	☐

Adding Two-Digit Numbers

Write the addition problem. Then find the sum.

1. Alan has 13 dinosaurs.
He gets 14 more.
How many dinosaurs does
he have in all?

Tens	Ones
1	3
+ 1	4
2	7

__27__ dinosaurs

---

2. Dee read 32 books last month.
She read 27 books this month.
How many books did Dee read
in 2 months?

Tens	Ones
+	

_____ books

---

3. Joan picks 35 apples.
She picks 13 pears.
How many apples and pears
does Joan pick in all?

Tens	Ones
+	

_____ apples and pears

Circle the number that solves the riddle.

4. I am greater than 37 + 10.
I have more tens than ones.
Which number am I?

5. I am less than 52 + 13.
I have more ones than tens.
Which number am I?

Regrouping in Addition

Write the addition problem. Then find the sum.

1. At the circus, Mark saw
   14 clowns in a wagon.
   He saw 5 clowns riding bikes.
   How many clowns did Mark see in all?

Tens	Ones
1	4
+	5
1	9

__19__ clowns

2. Kim Lee saw 26 elephants
   march into the ring.
   7 more elephants followed them.
   How many elephants were there in all?

Tens	Ones
+	

_____ elephants

3. Rob saw 15 lions and 8 tigers.
   How many lions and tigers
   did Rob see in all?

Tens	Ones
+	

_____ lions and tigers

Use the number line to add.

```
<---+----+----+----+----+----+----+----+----+----+----+--->
   45   46   47   48   49   50   51   52   53   54   55
```

4. 48 + 3 = _____   5. 46 + 7 = _____

Exact Answer or Estimate?

Kevin wants to buy a bag of nuts.

It costs 27¢.

Kevin has a quarter and 3 dimes.

Does he have enough money?

Do we need an exact answer or an estimate?

Read the problem again. What facts does it tell you?

Kevin has 1 quarter and 3 dimes.

He needs 27¢.

Think: A quarter is worth $\underset{\cdots\cdots\cdots}{25}$ ¢.

Add 1 dime to get $\underset{\cdots\cdots\cdots}{35}$ ¢. 35 ¢ ⊘ 27¢

Kevin has 2 more dimes. He has enough money.

I do not need to find an exact answer.

An estimate will solve the problem.

Check.

Circle **exact answer** or **estimate**.

1. Dinner will be ready in 1 hour.
   Kevin has 3 chores to do.
   Each chore will take 10 minutes.
   Can Kevin finish his chores before dinner?

   exact answer   estimate

Using the page Help children *read and understand* by asking them what facts they know about the problem and what they must find out. Help them determine whether they need an exact answer or an estimate.

Subtracting Groups of 10

Write the missing numbers.
Then complete the rule for each table.

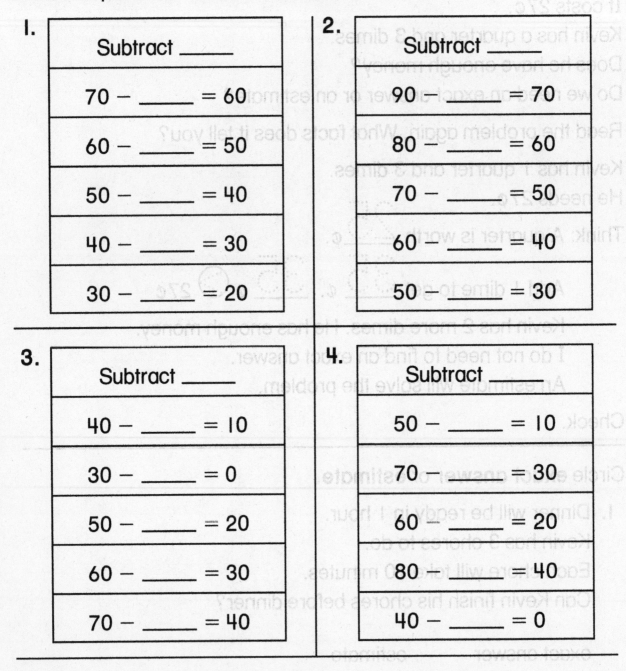

1.

Subtract _____
70 – _____ = 60
60 – _____ = 50
50 – _____ = 40
40 – _____ = 30
30 – _____ = 20

2.

Subtract _____
90 – _____ = 70
80 – _____ = 60
70 – _____ = 50
60 – _____ = 40
50 – _____ = 30

3.

Subtract _____
40 – _____ = 10
30 – _____ = 0
50 – _____ = 20
60 – _____ = 30
70 – _____ = 40

4.

Subtract _____
50 – _____ = 10
70 – _____ = 30
60 – _____ = 20
80 – _____ = 40
40 – _____ = 0

Solve.

5. Alex buys an apple and an orange for 80¢.

   The orange costs 50¢.

   How much did the apple cost? _____ ¢

Subtracting Tens from Two-Digit Numbers

The school is having a book fair.
Write a subtraction sentence. Solve.

1. There are 35 picture books.
10 picture books are sold.
How many books are left?

_____ – _____ = _____

_____ picture books

2. There are 41 dinosaur books.
20 of them are sold. How
many dinosaur books are left?

_____ – _____ = _____

_____ dinosaur books

3. Tanya has 68¢. She buys
a book about horses for 40¢.
How much does she
have left?

_____ ¢ – _____ ¢ = _____ ¢

_____ ¢

4. There are 79 books on
a table. The first graders
buy 60 of them. How many
books are left?

_____ – _____ = _____

_____ books

5. Answer the question.

Tim says that 55 – 40 = 95. Is he correct? Explain.

_____

_____

Subtracting Two-Digit Numbers

Write the subtraction problem.
Then find the difference.

1. Marco has 29 trading cards.
   He gives 14 of them to a friend.
   How many trading cards does
   Marco have left?

Tens	Ones

   _____ trading cards

2. Sherry has 45 shells.
   She uses 13 to make a
   picture frame. How many
   shells does she have left?

Tens	Ones

   _____ shells

3. On her birthday, Candace brings
   38 cupcakes to school.
   The children in her class eat 36 cupcakes.
   How many cupcakes are left?

Tens	Ones

   _____ cupcakes

4. Write the missing numbers.
   Then write the next subtraction problem in the pattern.

   76   66   56   ☐   ☐   ☐

   $$\begin{array}{r} \\ -\ 10 \\ \hline \end{array}$$
   $$\begin{array}{r} \boxed{} \\ -\ 10 \\ \hline 56 \end{array}$$
   $$\begin{array}{r} \\ -\ 10 \\ \hline \boxed{} \end{array}$$
   $$\begin{array}{r} \\ -\ 10 \\ \hline 36 \end{array}$$
   $$\begin{array}{r} \\ -\ 10 \\ \hline 26 \end{array}$$
   $$\begin{array}{r} \boxed{} \\ -\ \boxed{} \\ \hline \boxed{} \end{array}$$

Regrouping in Subtraction

Write the subtraction problem. Then find the difference.

1. There are 33 grapes.

   John eats 5 grapes.

   How many grapes are left?

	Tens	Ones
−		

   _____ grapes

2. Angel has 58 pennies.

   He uses 6 pennies to buy a muffin.

   How many pennies does he have left?

	Tens	Ones
−		

   _____ pennies

3. Susie has 60 socks.

   She throws away 8 socks

   because they have holes.

   How many socks does

   Susie have left?

	Tens	Ones
−		

   _____ socks

4. Draw the missing cubes.

PROBLEM-SOLVING STRATEGY
Make a Graph

The first grade has 3 soccer teams.

Which team scored the most goals?

Goals Scored

	Game 1	Game 2	Game 3	Game 4
Orange Team	10	10	10	10
Yellow Team	20	10	20	10
Red Team	10	10	10	20

The chart shows how many goals each team scored.

We want to find which team scored the most goals.

Use the information in the chart to make a graph.

Color one box for every ten goals.

Goals Scored

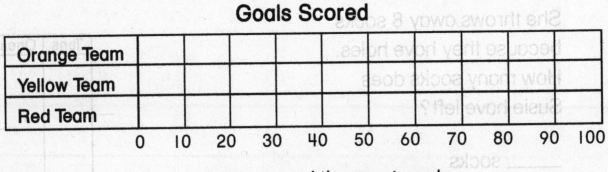

The _____ team scored the most goals.

Check your answer. Make sure you colored the

correct number of boxes.

Writing in Math

1. Write another question that could be answered using the graph.

_____

Using the page To help children **plan and solve,** ask them what they must find and how making the graph would help them solve the problem. Have children complete the graph to solve.

Name _____

Caring For Kittens

There were 26 cats at the animal shelter. 12 cats
were adopted. How many cats were left?
You can write a subtraction sentence to solve. $\underline{26} - \underline{12} = \underline{14}$

There were 14 cats left.

How can we be sure the answer is correct?
We can write a related addition sentence to
check our subtraction. Our answer is correct. $\underline{12} + \underline{14} = \underline{26}$

---

1. Tony brings 19 old towels and 6 dishes to the animal shelter.
   How many items did he bring in all?

   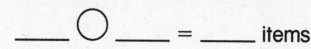

   _____ ◯ _____ = _____ items

2. There are 48 cans of cat food on the shelf.
   There are 20 cans of cat food in a box.
   How many cans of cat food are there in all?

   _____ ◯ _____ = _____ cans

Writing in Math

3. Flor buys a toy mouse for 27¢. She buys a cat collar
   for 52¢. Does she have to regroup to find out how
   much the items will cost altogether? Explain.

   _____

   _____

Using the page Ask children to *look back and check* the problems. Have them make sure that their answers
make sense. Have them check their addition and subtraction.